# THE SOUTH HAMS COAST

gerry miles

HALSGROVE

*for Maureen*

## Acknowledgements

I am indebted to a number of people for their invaluable support, encouragement and assistance, without whom this book would never have become a reality.
My wife Maureen for her love, patience and understanding in giving me the space, time and freedom to realise my ambitions. Jane and Graham Price at The Mayne Gallery for having faith in my art and promoting and exhibiting my paintings. My son Justin for guiding me through the complexities of desktop publishing. Simon Butler at Halsgrove Publishers, for committing to print and market this book based upon my original concept and for giving me sound and professional advise throughout the project.



First published in Great Britain in 2008



British Library Cataloguing-in-Publication Data.
A CIP record for this title is available from the British Library.

ISBN 978 1 84114 690 4

Halsgrove
Halsgrove House
Ryelands Industrial Estate
Bagley Road, Wellington
Somerset TA21 9PZ
Tel : 01823 653 777
Fax : 01823 216 796
e-mail : sales@halsgrove.com
website : www.halsgrove.com

Printed by D'Auria Industrie Grafiche Spa, Italy

# CONTENTS

Hope Cove

## INTRODUCTION

There are some places where you simply feel at home and when I first visited the South Hams in 1975 I was immediately captivated by its charm and beauty. My discovery of the area was as if I had stumbled upon a treasured spot that time had passed by.

I came as a diver to explore the many shipwrecks that litter the seabed along the rugged coastline and to delight in scenic diving on kelp-clad reefs that disappear into the clear waters off the headlands. During subsequent holidays, being avid walkers, my wife Maureen and I trekked along miles of the coastal path taking in the breathtaking views and exploring the lovely beaches, coves and estuaries. We took great pleasure in visiting and becoming acquainted with the historic towns and picturesque old-world villages. It seemed a natural progression upon retirement for us to set up a home in Hope Cove at the heart of this remarkable coastal region

Retirement from a life in international business presented me with new challenges and opportunities. Having studied and practised landscape painting and drawing all my life, I decided to combine my artistic talents with my other keen interests in photography and hiking, from which the embryo of the idea for this book took shape. I set out to create my own personal record of the South Hams Coast, as I experienced it at the turn of the century, in a series of landscape paintings and pencil studies. After much deliberation, I decided that the best vehicle for this purpose would be carefully chosen circular walks that would provide a framework for the illustrations. Although at times the challenge seemed somewhat daunting, the subject was so inspirational that it drove me onwards.

In 1960 the South Hams coastal region was designated an area of outstanding natural beauty (AONB) and was later awarded the title of South Devon Heritage Coast by the Countryside Agency in 1984. Large tracts of this coast and coastal farmland are owned by The National Trust whose objective is to preserve them for future generations and to protect them from commercial development. English Heritage conserves and manages many historic monuments in the area and there are numerous locations designated as Sites of Special Scientific Interest (SSSI). In consideration of these important programmes and other actions targeted at improving the natural environment, such as the Countryside Stewardship Schemes, you could be forgiven for thinking that the South Hams is preserved in aspic. There is no denying the vital importance of protecting the natural beauty of this most English of landscapes, together with the social, agricultural, industrial and marine heritage of the South Hams, but change is inevitable.

This book portrays a moment in time and I have some concerns about elements that may affect the future character of the region.

As a diver I have witnessed the sad decline in what was once a rich and varied marine life in the shallow coastal waters. Modern fishing methods and techniques have resulted in the wholesale plunder of the sea, necessitating the introduction of fishing quotas. The depletion of fish stocks and fishing restrictions has seen the demise of an industry that was once so influential in shaping the coastal towns and villages of the South Hams. Boatyards have disappeared and wharves transformed into luxury apartments. In agriculture, mechanisation, growing international competition and market pressures from supermarkets, together with sweeping changes in agricultural policies sees fewer people working on the land. Are there any barns left in the South Hams yet to be converted? Social pressures have been mounting due to second home ownership and holiday lets that have inflated the housing market and altered the profile of the community. There is an ever increasing dependency upon tourism and leisure activities in the area that puts pressure upon local amenities. Thinking further ahead, global warming is already creating extreme weather conditions that may accelerate coastal erosion and, in future, searches for replenishable alternatives to fossil fuels could see the introduction of wind farms and tidal energy projects.

Looking at it objectively, I do not suppose that in the past local people were too enamoured with the denuding of the woodlands to supply timber for shipbuilding, or the excavation of hillsides and moorland for clay, slate and stone. The "scars" of the past such as limekilns, stone quarries, coastal fortifications, quays, wharves and sea defences are now an integral part of this treasured landscape and coastline. Dare I suggest that some modern changes may at some distant date become cherished features of the South Hams?

An illustrated guide must be full of pictorial images and there was no better way for me to convey my personal impressions of this wonderful coastline than through my artwork. These landscape paintings express my interpretation of what I find outstanding about the natural beauty of the area. My perception is not restricted to the charm of the scenes themselves, but includes the moods created by the pervading light and the changes in atmosphere throughout the seasons. I wanted the text of the book to be punctuated by pencil studies depicting things that typify the South Hams and showing people enjoying what the area has to offer. In order to enhance my collection of images still further, I hit upon the idea of taking to the air and made helicopter flights, filming and photographing the whole length of the coast between the Dart and the Yealm. In this way I was able to develop aerial views of the coast upon which the walking routes could be superimposed, thus providing a different perspective and a more comprehensive overview. I hope that the aerial pictures, coupled with colourful walking maps and detailed route descriptions, may encourage readers to venture out along the South West Coast Path and the footpaths and bridleways to experience first-hand the marvels of the South Hams.

Nature takes its course and the struggle goes on between those who would keep the South Hams exactly the way it is, those who have ideas to improve it and those with plans to exploit it. Whatever your particular interests, I trust that you will derive as much pleasure and enjoyment from the South Hams as I do and that you will find it in you to safeguard and hold dear its unique and irreplaceable riches.

*Gerry Miles*

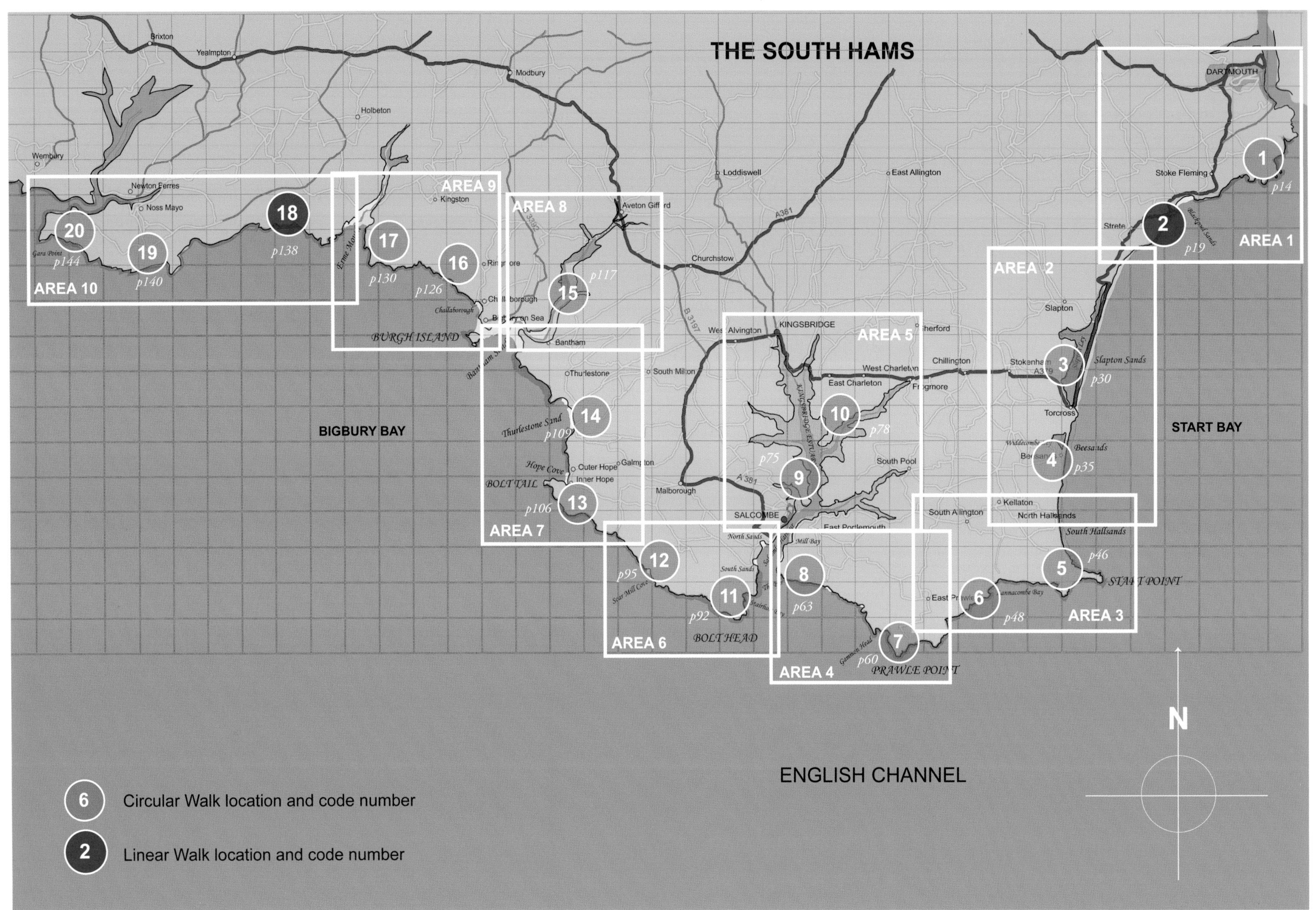




KEY MAP TO SOUTH HAMS COAST

# USING THE GUIDE

## Scope

This illustrated guide covers the south coast of Devon from the River Dart in the east to the River Yealm in the west. These rivers mark the boundaries of the coastal region known as the South Hams. Although the guide concentrates on the coastline, it includes the river estuaries and the countryside immediately inland along the recommended circular walks.

The South Hams coast has been divided into 10 areas as shown on the Key Map on the opposite page and the numbers of these areas correspond with the 10 sections of the book that are arranged in sequence from east to west. The Key Map shows the location of 18 circular walks and 2 linear walks that have been carefully selected to give a comprehensive coverage of the entire coastline.

Each of the 10 sections of the book includes:

- Landscape paintings and pencil drawings illustrating that area of the coast.
- A coastal description explaining its natural characteristics.
- A profile of every beach and cove that is accessible from the South West Coast Path.
- Aerial maps, walking maps and route descriptions for the recommended circular walks.
- Information about special landmarks and natural features.
- Historical notes and points of interest.

## Aerial Maps

Each walking route has been superimposed upon an aerial picture to give an exceptional overview of the coast, countryside and terrain that will be encountered on the walk. The route is shown as a bold yellow dotted line with white arrows suggesting the best direction to be followed. The aerial map should be used in conjunction with the walking map.

## Walking Maps

The walking maps are derived from the Ordnance Survey Explorer Map OL20 and grid reference numbers are shown for ease of correlation. The walking route is marked by a broad yellow band and the style of the line along the route denotes whether that part of the walk is on the coastal path, footpath or bridleway, farm track or country lane. The red arrows give the direction of the walk corresponding to the route description, chosen to give the best views.

A legend of symbols is given in this section to help in interpreting the maps and to give the location of car parks, public toilets, public houses, restaurants, cafés and tearooms.

Decision points along the walk are marked alphabetically and are highlighted in the route descriptions by circled letters.

The location of beaches and coves are shown as circled numbers and these numbers correspond with the profiles described under "Accessible Beaches and Coves" in that section of the book.

The walk reference numbers for the circular walks are displayed on the maps in a light blue circle; the linear walks are shown in a dark blue circle.

All maps are oriented due north as given by the compass rose.

## Route Descriptions

Care has been taken to avoid ambiguity and to give precise directions using signposts, waymarkers and permanent landmarks. Signposts are susceptible to damage and replacement of course, but these are rigorously maintained by the South Hams District Council and The National Trust. A description of the views, the nature of the trail at each step of the way and other observations should help to dispel any confusion.

The walks have been tried and tested on several occasions by

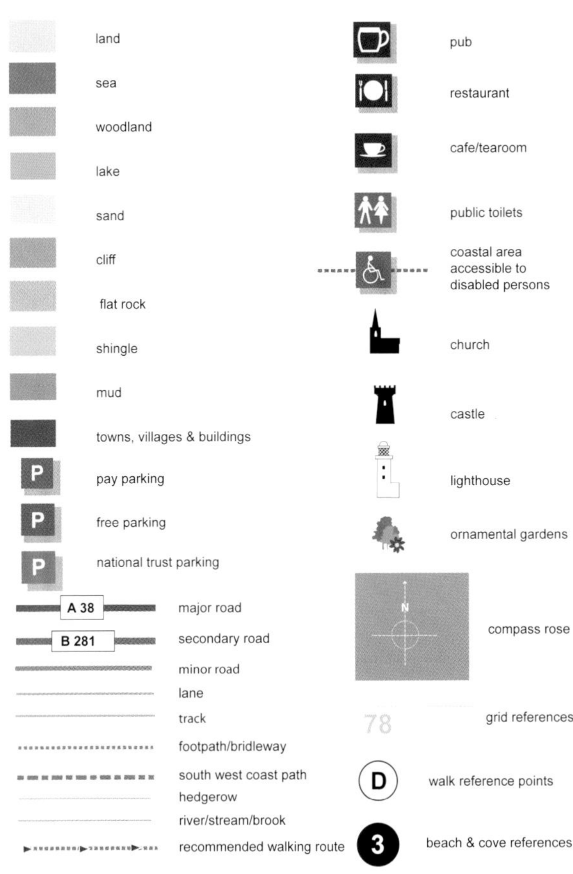


WALKING MAP SYMBOLS

people armed only with the walking map and route description and they all appear to be straightforward to follow. You do not have to be an expert in orienteering and should be able to venture out with confidence.

## The Walks

The chosen circular walks can be completed within a morning or an afternoon provided you are reasonably fit and agile. The estimated times allow for stops to admire the views, take photographs, get your breath back and take care of the calls of nature. The young and energetic will have no difficulty in improving on these times. If caught out by inclement weather, fatigue or illness, all footpaths and lanes that could prove useful as a short cut have been included on the walking maps.

It is not difficult to combine some of the adjacent walks to extend the hike.

The walks have been graded to give an indication as to the obstacles encountered en-route.

- Grade 1 Easy gradients. No stiles. Firm paths.
- Grade 2 Medium gradients. Stiles, Firm paths.
- Grade 3 Steep gradients. Stiles. Rocky and uneven sections.

Alternative car parks are shown. Circular walks can be started at any convenient place. The alphabetic symbols will help to pick up the route description at the appropriate spot.

The location of hotels, pubs, restaurants, cafés and tearooms should not be taken as a recommendation; this is not a good food guide but simply shows where refreshments are available. Some cafés and tearooms are seasonal.

**Compact Disc**

This guide is intended as a reference book and is too large and cumbersome to take on a walk. A CD is available with all of the aerial maps, walking maps and route descriptions for the 20 walks. A4 prints of individual walks can be made on an ink-jet printer and discarded after the walk if the pages become soiled or wet.

The CD costs £5.00 including post and packaging (U.K. only) and can be ordered from the author's website at **www.devonpaint.nl** Simply click the CD button on the opening page of the website and follow the instructions.

**Accessibility**

The accessibility of beaches and coves from the South West Coast Path have also been graded and great care must be taken when descending to any beach or foreshore. They all have recognisable paths and tracks but the more difficult ones are steep and worn into the cliff face by constant use over the years. Often sea erosion at the base of the cliff makes the last section troublesome.

- Access Level 1 Easy path. Steps or slipway. Backed by a car park.
- Access Level 2 Easy path. Steps or slipway. Involves walking along the coastal path.
- Access Level 3 Low cliff. (less than 50 feet.) Steep path or steps or a combination of both.
- Access Level 4 High cliff. Steep path. Remote.

Safety tips for Access Level 4:

- Do not go down into a cove unless you are absolutely certain that you are capable of climbing back.
- The paths are sand, gravel and rock so wear sturdy footwear that gives a good grip.
- If there is no beach at high water, check the state of the tide.
- Keep a constant watch on the flood tide to avoid getting cut off from the return path once you are on the beach.
- Carry your belongings in a rucksack so that you have both hands free.
- Do not descend into deep and remote coves alone. A twisted ankle or broken leg could prove fatal. It is most likely that there is no mobile phone signal!
- Take care on the descent and the climb back not to dislodge stones or rocks that could injure people below.

**Safe Bathing**

Any statements in this book indicating that there is safe bathing from any beach or cove can only be taken as a general guideline. The responsibility for safety when entering the water rests with the individual and will be dependent upon the competence of the swimmer and the prevailing sea conditions. On beaches where there are no RNLI Lifeguards in attendance, life-buoys can often be found tethered to posts at the back of the beach. These are only useful if there are other people on the beach capable of offering assistance.

**The Countryside Code**

All conservation starts with a responsible attitude and if a commonsense code of conduct is followed when visiting the coast and countryside then it will be left in a good state for others to enjoy and there will be minimum inconvenience and disturbance to those that live and work there.

**Dogs**

With the exception of walk 14, where there are difficulties with stiles, dogs can be taken on all of the walks. However, dogs are not welcome on many of the popular bathing beaches and wherever there are notices prohibiting dogs or insistence that dogs be kept on the lead, they should be strictly observed.

Dog owners should take particular care to clean up any fouling on the coastal path and footpaths.

# 1 DARTMOUTH TO STRETE

▲ **Dartmouth Royal Regatta - 2006**

HMS 'Mercury', an offshore patrol vessel, and HMS 'Sir Belvedere', a Royal Fleet Auxiliary, rest at anchor in the River Dart during the Regatta. The number of yachts and other boats moored in the harbour is swelled by hundreds of visiting craft.

**The Inner Harbour and Quay**

## DARTMOUTH

Dartmouth is the quintessential Devon coastal town that is quaint and picturesque. It is steeped in history and is rich in architecture as well as being a deep-water port long associated with sea trading and naval exploits.

In summer the town's embankments and narrow streets bustle with tourists who not only enjoy what the town has to offer, but crowd on to pleasure boats and ferries to explore the tidal waters of the Dart. They can sail out to the river mouth, upstream to the market town of Totnes, or cross the river to Kingswear on the opposite shore.

There is a wealth of restaurants and cafés to suit every budget and taste in the labyrinth of streets, quays and embankments that make up the town centre, and in Foss Street and Market Street souvenir shops vie with art galleries for the visitor's attention.

**Ducks in the Sun - Totnes** ►

These wharves are at the limits of the navigable channel of the River Dart, relics of a time when barges plied the river between Dartmouth and Totnes.

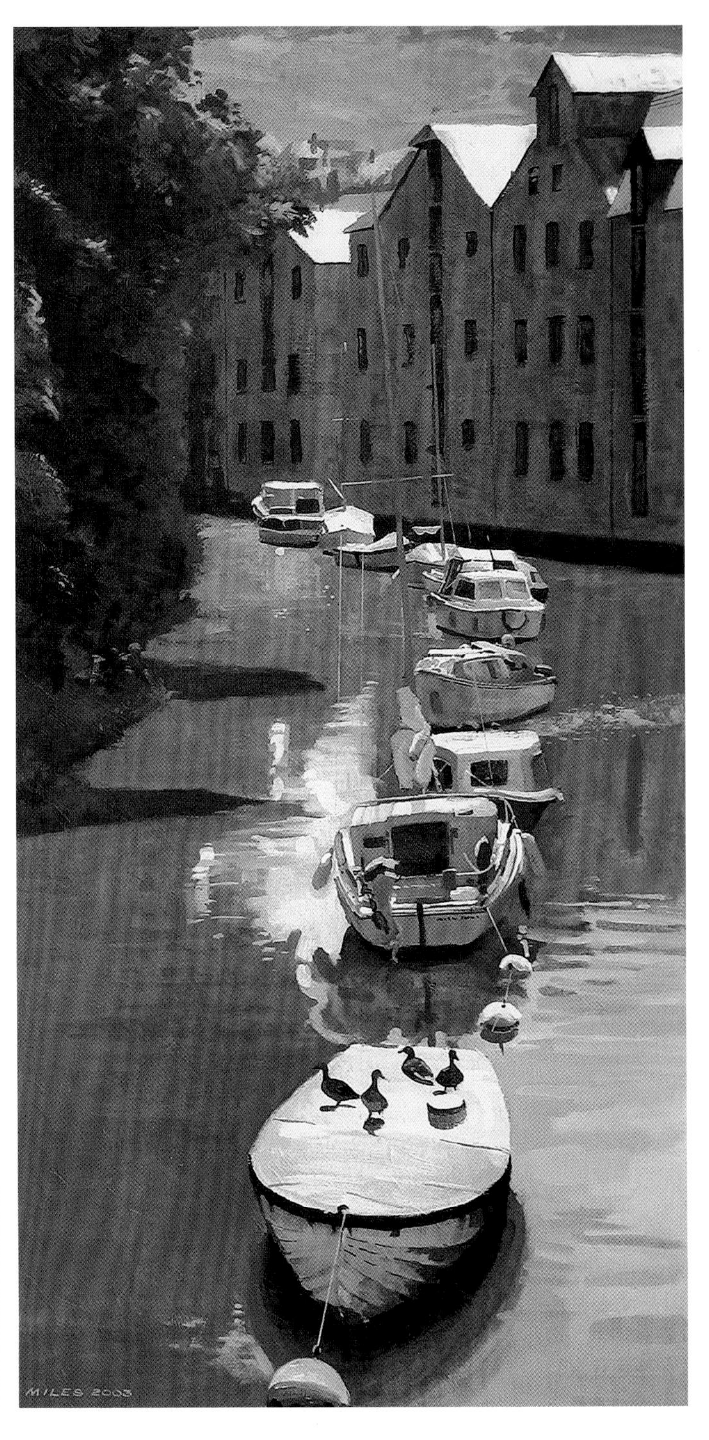

**The Butterwalk**

Rivalry between wealthy merchant families in the 18th and 19th century resulted in the richness and variety of Dartmouth's architecture and its fine harbour facilities. These dignitaries contended to outdo each other in public works to gain prominence in the town. Of earlier architecture, a few Tudor buildings remain and the beautifully restored Butterwalk in Duke Street, built in 1635, is a unique example of a timber-framed arcade mounted on granite pillars.

Dartmouth Castle was purpose-designed to house gun batteries to defend the town and port from foreign marauders. These defences were reinforced by a smaller circular fort that stands on the waterfront at Bayard's Cove.

The imposing edifice of the Britannia Royal Naval College overlooks the town and since 1905 renowned naval officers, including such eminent cadets as King George V, King George VI, the Duke of Edinburgh and Prince Charles, received their initial training here. This seal of respectability is a far cry from the flagrant piracy and privateering that emanated from Dartmouth in the 13th. Century.

The town has never been connected by a main road and although there is limited parking, the narrow streets and quaysides cannot cope with the volume of modern-day traffic. A park-and ride service takes the strain and stress out of a day's visit for the motorist. The railway did not reach the town either, even though a railway station stands on the embankment at the town quay. The original plans had a railway bridge spanning the Dart, but overwhelming local protest scrapped the scheme. The station had already been built when it was decided to terminate the railway at Kingswear. Daily excursions link Dartmouth with Kingswear, Paignton and Totnes by ferry, steam train, open-top bus and river cruise in a delightful round-robin tour.

The major event of the year is the annual Royal Regatta in August when the town fills to overflowing and the Red Arrows perform their spectacular flying display above the awe-struck crowds. Visiting naval vessels anchor in mid-stream and a myriad of colourful sailing boats compete for challenge trophies. The inevitable firework display lights the night sky, illuminating a town that has managed to preserve its old world charm.

## THE COASTLINE

The east facing hillsides above Dartmouth are sheltered from the prevailing westerly winds as evidenced by their densely wooded slopes that reach down to the water's edge along the Dart Estuary. From Dartmouth

**Bayard's Cove** ▲

The small circular battery of Bayard's Cove Fort was built around 1509 and the houses on this oldest of Dartmouth's quays are also Tudor. A plaque commemorates a visit to this quay by the Pilgrim Fathers in 1620 who stopped here to repair their ships and to take on provisions. What better on a warm, sunny day than to sit on one of the wooden benches, stretch your legs out across the cobbles and watch the busy river traffic on the Dart?

Castle out to Blackstone Point at the mouth of the river, the low lying rock cliffs have been etched into small coves but trees still fringe the clifftops, diminishing to scrub out towards the exposed headland.

From Blackstone Point to Compass Cove the grassy downs are protected from serious erosion by a low, flat bed of rock that runs along the full length of the shoreline. Although split by ravines and gullies, this rock buttress creates an effective sea defence.

In contrast, Compass Cove is cut deep into the hillside, below where the contours of the land form a steep grass valley. High cliffs range up on its western flank, getting steeper around the escarpments of Willow Cove and Shinglehill Cove, becoming most commanding at Combe Point.

Cliff top walking is interrupted between Warren Point and Blackpool Sands and the Ordnance Survey map shows the coastal path routed on roads through the village of Stoke Fleming. This is effectively a break in the coastal path and occurs also to a lesser extent at Strete. Fortunately these are the only two hindrances in the entire length of the South Hams coastline.

Beyond the beautiful crescent beach of Blackpool Sands that stands at the head of an attractive wooded valley, the cliffs below Strete begin to diminish and then melt into the low, long sweep of Slapton Sands.

## ACCESSIBLE BEACHES AND COVES

### 1. Sugary Cove.

(Access Level 2)

Sugary Cove is a short walk from Dartmouth Castle and is a bit of a mystery in that it does not appear on the Ordnance Survey map. At the top of the bank above the Castle car park you take the path to the left. This goes down through trees past a grass picnic area equipped with tables and benches and then descends to some wide steps. The footpath curves around the back of the cove and in the middle, a wooden stairway drops right down to the beach. Sugary Cove was struck off the list of Devon bathing beaches in 2004 due to difficulty of access, but the new steps have seen it reopened. The adjoining Castle Cove is not so lucky; at the time of writing it remains closed due to a small landslide.

Sugary Cove has no beach at high water and is a mixture of sand, shingle and bedrock with large boulders lying under the low cliff at the back. The cove is very secluded with trees overhanging the cliff top.

You can return to the coastal path via an alternative zigzag track.

### 2. Compass Cove

(Access Level 4)

The coastal path passes close to the top of Compass Cove where there is a stile and bench at the intersection with the track down to the beach. Compass Cove is reachable down a series of well-made, robust steps that at one point drop as a vertical ladder from a cantilevered platform, thus restricting the descent to the fit and agile.

At the bottom of the last flight of stone steps a life-buoy hangs on a post attached to a coiled, nylon rope.

The steeply sloping beach is of coarse sand with rivulets running across it and no beach remains at high tide. Stone walling at the back of the beach is breaking away as earlier attempts to stem the progress of erosion succumbs to the tireless pounding of the waves. The sand goes out for about 50 yards and this beach is good for swimming when the sea is quiet.

In winter, grey seals have often been observed close to the beach.

### 3. Blackpool Sands

(Access Level 1)

This is a private beach with a 2½ miles stretch of coarse sand and shingle in a picturesque setting just off the A379 in a valley that lies mid-way between Strete and Stoke Fleming. Cliffs on either side flank the beach and trees separate the beach from the road. There is a bus stop in both directions at the entrance.

A stream flows out onto the south side of the beach forming a large fresh water pool in the sand. This stream that courses down the valley separates the parishes of Strete and Blackawton and the resulting pond is thought to have given the beach its name.

Families with small children are well catered for with all the facilities for a day at the seaside immediately to hand. These include a large pay car park at the rear of the beach, a café with a seated terrace arranged under large umbrellas, a beach shop, and watersports

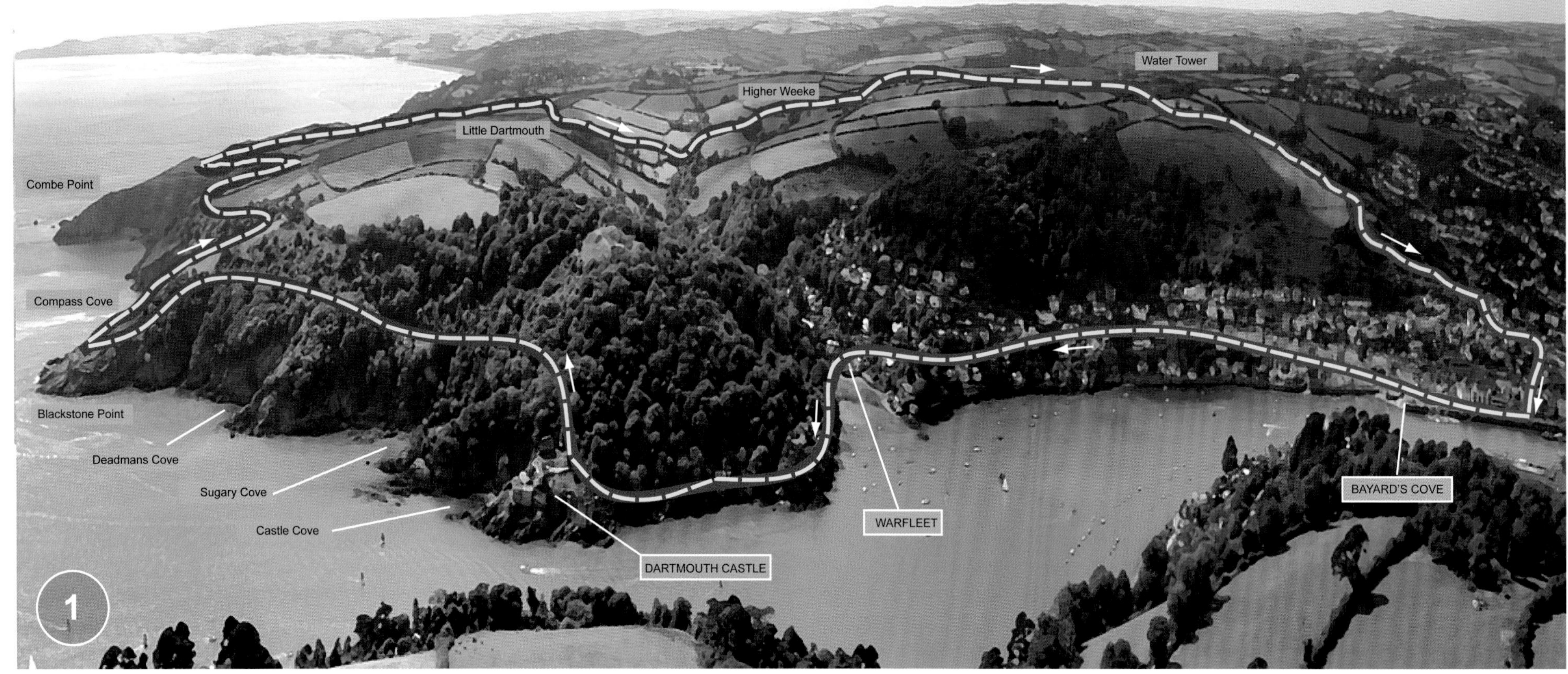


hire of kayaks and surf boards. Sand Pits are provided on the beach in front of the car park for the avid sand castle builders. Public toilets and telephones complete the picture.

This is a Blue Flag beach with lifeguards in attendance during the summer months and good access and special facilities for the disabled.

No dogs are allowed on the beach under any circumstances

**4. Forest Cove**

(Access Level 3)

At high water this cove is but a small patch of gravel and coarse sand but as the tide recedes it becomes far more impressive, and it is possible to walk along the seashore to Landcombe Cove below Matthew's Point, where steps from the hotel above are cut into the rock face. The shingle is banked high against cliffs of shining flat plates of mica schist with one or two small caves at the base. Although the beach shelves steeply swimming is quite safe. However, you must keep an eye on the tide; if you were careless it would be very easy to get cut off.

## WALK 1 DARTMOUTH CASTLE

**Distance** **5 miles**
**Time** **3¼ hours**
**Grade** **3**

The walk starts from The National Trust car park at Little Dartmouth. **(A)**

To reach this car park take the A379 to Stoke Fleming and then the B3205 to Dartmouth Castle. The first minor road to the right is signposted to Little Dartmouth.

Leave the car park and take the lane to Little Dartmouth Farm ¼ mile. Walk straight through the farm and out the other side to a row of houses on the left where you find a footpath to Weeke Cottage ½ mile. This is a wide farm track that does a small chicane at the crest of the hill before heading down into a valley. After passing through two five bar gates the driveway to the cottage runs out to a lane where you turn left up the hill. **(B)**

A footpath immediately on the right is signposted to Swannaton ¼ mile and a boulder at the entrance bears the name Higher Weeke. At the group of houses at

Higher Weeke a waymarker directs you past a barn and a bungalow after which the bridleway carries on as a grass track. Hoof prints in the mud shows that it is regularly used and the track tends to be wet and sticky in the winter months due to the run-off from the fields. Carry on along the bridleway up the hill to the next road.

Going left up the hill you come to a triangular junction with the A379. **(C)** A house stands in the middle and at the 40 mph sign you turn right along the back of the house and again right into the main road.

After 20 yards a lane on the right is signposted to the Recycling Centre which heads out to a large, grey water tower. At the Amenity Site take the lane with the warning sign "No vehicle except for agricultural access", this is Jawbone Lane that descends into the heart of Dartmouth.

When you pass the ruins of Jawbone Barn the lane gets steeper and you get the first glimpse of the River Dart, and you may see the upper car ferry chugging its way back and forth. The Britannia Royal Naval College appears across the valley to the left through occasional breaks in the high banks and stone walling.

At the place where two footpaths branch off to the right to Dyer's Wood and Ditcham Steps, there is a marvellous view over the rooftops of Dartmouth away to Kingswear and out to the river mouth and Dartmouth Castle. **(D)**

Continue down Jawbones Hill and then right into Crowther's Hill where the old gabled houses start to overhang and crowd the street. At Above Town Road turn right and then directly left down Horn Hill Steps and just where they cross Higher Street, stop to admire the timber framed Tudor frontage of The Cherub Inn.

**The Cherub Inn**

Thought to date from 1380, the Cherub Inn that stands on the corner of Horn Hill Steps and Higher Street lays claim to being Dartmouth's oldest building. It is now off the beaten track but in Tudor times Higher Street was an important thoroughfare. In the course of time fire and bombs have ravaged the street but although left derelict until its restoration in 1958, The Cherub still retains many of its original features. This beautiful building is now a pub and restaurant.

Walk out to the embankment from the bottom of the next flight of steps and proceed down river along the promenade past the Harbour Office until you reach the large cannon facing out across the river. **(E)** The road around to Bayard's Cove passes the slip road to the Lower Ferry.

Entering Bayard's Cove you would be forgiven for thinking that you had stepped on to a film set.

**Bayard's Cove**

The cobbled quayside at Bayard's Cove evokes images of sailing vessels and it is not difficult to imagine the Pilgrim Fathers on the 20th August 1620 slipping their moorings on the 'Mayflower' and 'Speedwell' to embark upon the next stage of their remarkable and momentous voyage to America.
Once the busy heart of Dartmouth's shipping trade, this wharf is now a charming tourist attraction.

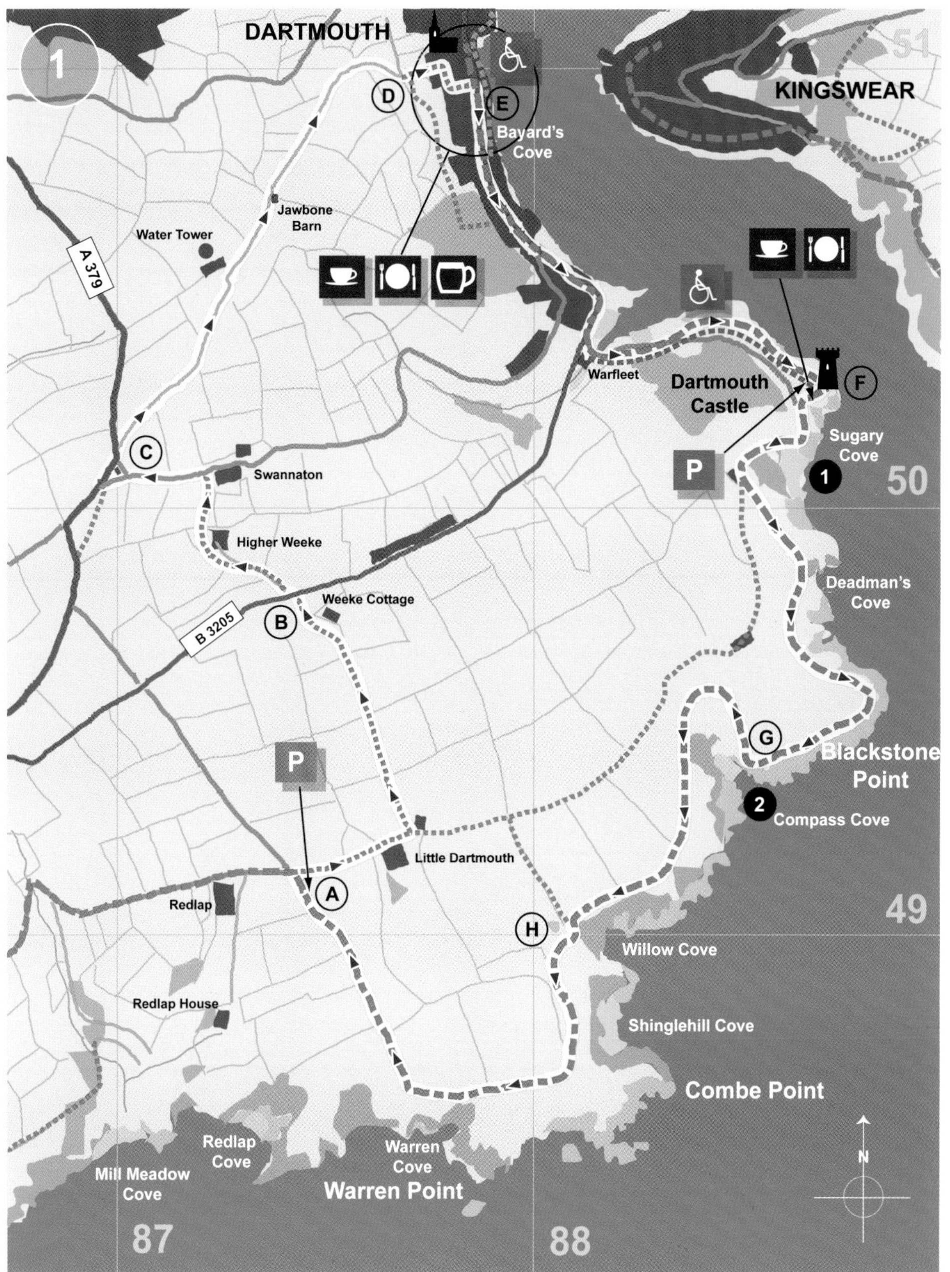

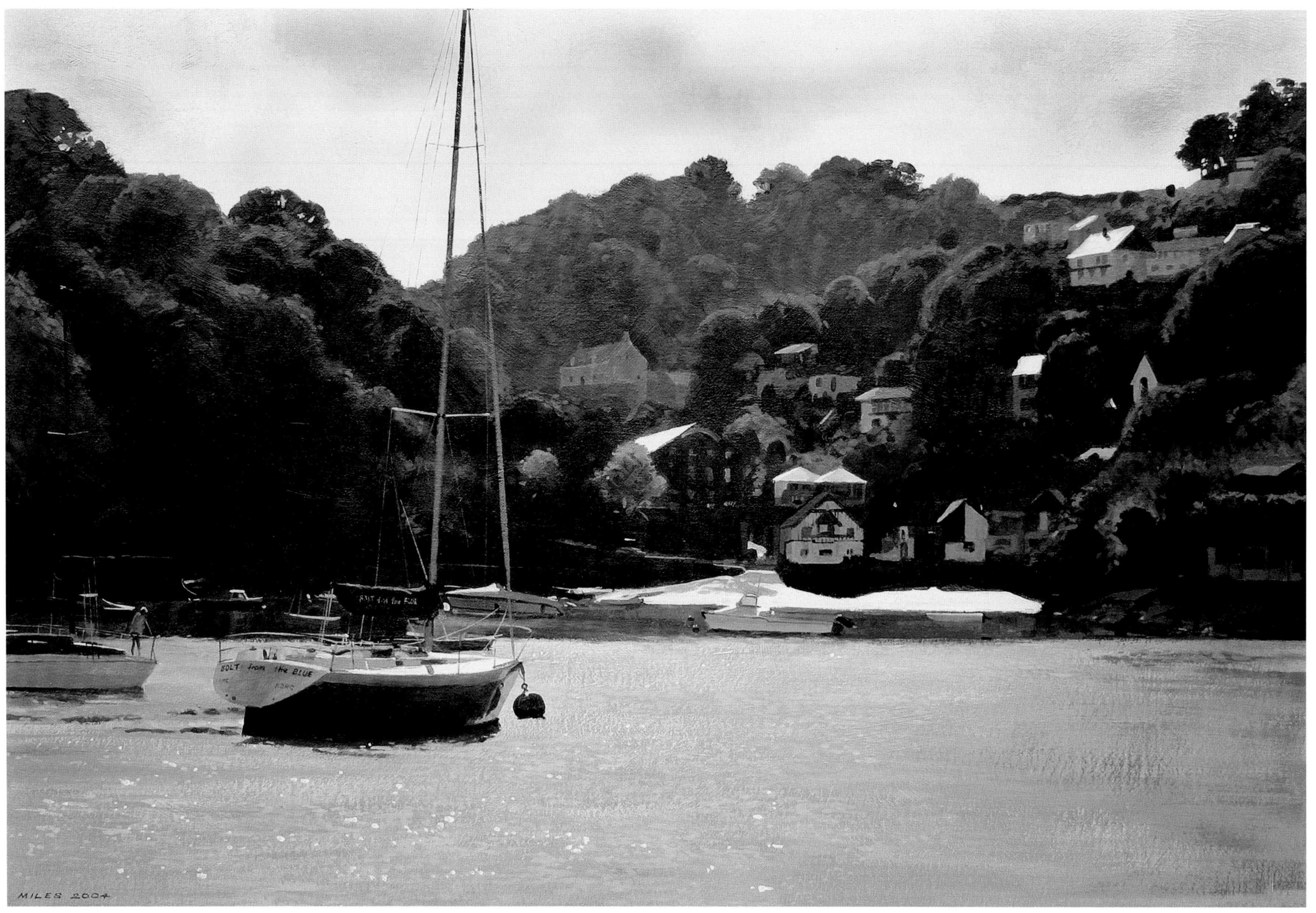


▲ **Warfleet**

Warfleet is a picturesque creek on the River Dart about half a mile south of Dartmouth town centre on the road leading to Dartmouth Castle. It has a sand and shingle foreshore and provides sheltered anchorage for small boats and yachts.

to an archway under the road and a slipway out to the small sand and gravel beach. From the beach a footpath brings you back to the road via a tiny, grassed park. Beyond Warfleet Creek take the left hand fork to St Petrox Church and Dartmouth Castle. **(F)**

Dartmouth Castle

**Dartmouth Castle**

Dartmouth Castle and Kingswear Castle face each other across the narrow entrance to the river Dart. They were built to protect ships and their cargoes moored in the deep-water harbour as well as the interests of wealthy merchants whose homes and warehouses ranged along the quays. From its conception Dartmouth Castle was purpose built to carry heavy guns and comprises a 15th century gun tower, a 19th century battery and guardroom, and gun emplacements ranged upon its walls. The castle appears quite imposing but it shares its rock platform with a white painted lighthouse and 17th Century, St Petrox Church that together add false elevation to the fortifications.

The earliest defences on this site, dating from 1388, consisted of a simple ditch and curtain wall built across the headland behind which soldiers, perhaps supported by stone throwing machines, could fire upon assailants attacking from the sea. In 1462 a heavy chain spanned the harbour mouth carried on small boats, but in 1481, the township, with the patronage of Edward IV, designed and built a castle strong enough to support heavy artillery. During the Napoleonic Wars the castle was modified to house the latest armament and even in 1940 a battery was built for a modern naval gun.

The castle is well preserved and is managed and maintained by English Heritage. It is open to the public all week from April to October and weekends from November to March.

**Warfleet Creek**

Down the ages Dartmouth has been the scene of large gatherings of warships. Under Richard the Lionheart, 37 ships left this port to join the second crusade in 1147. Flotillas of fighting ships launched surprise attacks along the French coast or joined blockades of French ports during the Napoleonic Wars, and the last fleet to gather here was assembled for the D-Day landings and the liberation of France in 1944. No guesses as to how Warfleet got its name!

It was a busy quay in its heyday with a ropewalk producing rigging, limekilns for fertilizer and later a mill that was diversely used for flour, papermaking, beer brewing and pottery. The last vestiges of industry have disappeared with the conversion of the old millhouse into apartments.

Beyond the cobbled quay of Bayard's Cove is a small fortress; you enter the fort, cross to the other side of the tower, stepping out under a low archway, and ascend the stairway to the road above.

This road with its narrow pavements rises away from the town towards Dartmouth Castle, and there are lovely views of Kingswear across the water. At the junction with Swannaton Road turn left into Castle Road and walk down to Warfleet Creek. At the head of the creek there are steps going down

After visiting the church and castle, climb the steps from the café and continue up the coastal path to Compass Cottage. A bridleway goes straight ahead to Little Dartmouth, but turn left taking the footpath through the woods out to Blackstone Point. Beyond a gate at the end of the woodland the path becomes uneven as it slopes down to the shoreline.

There are several tracks that branch off to the right but keep heading down to where the path comes out above the rocky foreshore. Eventually you come to a wooden footbridge over a deep ravine and a series of steps up to a stile above Compass Cove. **(G)**

Now begins the most taxing climb of the walk straight up the grass valley ahead. Thankfully someone has had the forethought to place a bench at the top where you can sit and get your breath back. From this resting place there follows a gentler slope to a gate after which the footpath skirts the clifftops of Willow Cove and Shinglehill Cove. These coves are not reachable from the coast path and in any case their boulder-strewn shores do not look very inviting. You pass a fenced-off pond that runs out through a culvert, the brook trickling down the hill and tumbling to the beach far below. **(H)**

Through a wide gap in a stone wall turn right and follow the wall to the top of the rise. The church at Stoke Fleming is straight ahead and you keep following the fence until you reach a kissing gate. The path then crosses three fields back to the car park.

## WALK 2 BLACKPOOL SANDS

**Distance** **1¼ miles**
**Time** **45 mins (one way)**
**Grade** **2**

Park carefully somewhere in the side streets of Strete.

The coast path is signposted from the main road in the middle of the village **(A)** and although it is not a circular route it is a very attractive short walk from Strete to Blackpool Sands. It is clearly signposted along its entire length initially taking you down into a narrow wooded valley spanned by a footbridge.

A gate brings you out into an open field and as you cross, impressive views of Start Bay come in to view above the treetops away to the right. Directly ahead is the headland of Matthew's Point surmounted by a hotel, beyond which the tip of the north end of Blackpool Sands can be seen.

Follow the line of waymarkers to the edge of the field and then go down a steep grass bank into the bottom of the valley that slopes away to the right to Forest Cove. The path then climbs up the other side to a gate at the top of the rise that leads out to the A379. **(B)**

Looking down the road a signpost on the opposite bank shows where the footpath resumes up steps and over a stile into a field. Walk along the hedgerow and cross the next field diagonally to a gateway in the far corner.

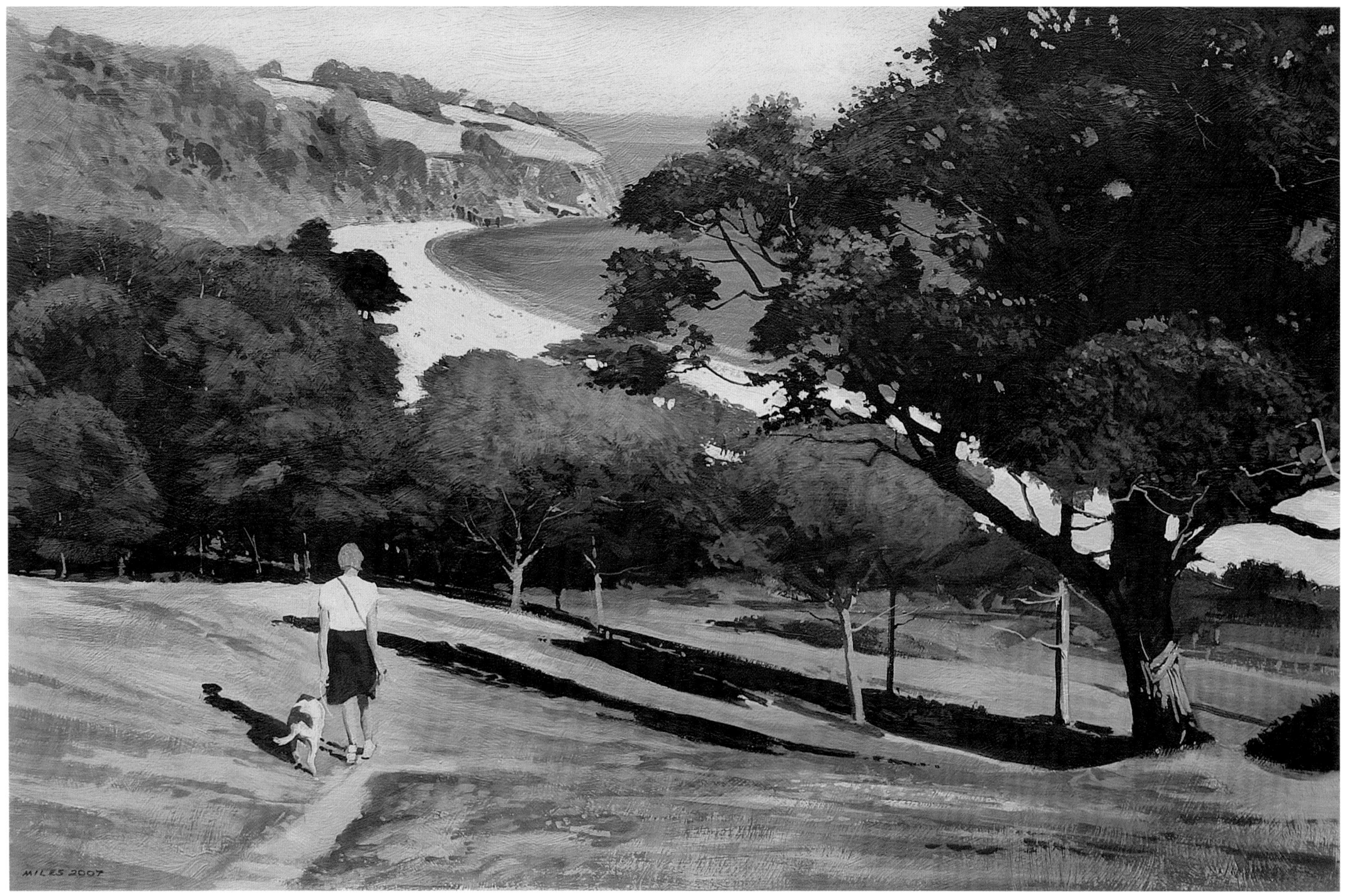


▲ **Blackpool Sands**

The wide beach of Blackpool Sands lies sheltered below wooded cliffs at the head of a secluded valley between Strete and Stoke Fleming. Although easily accessed on the busy coastal road, the peaceful charm of this picturesque spot can best be enjoyed by walking along the quiet paths and bridleways that thread their way across the fields from Strete.

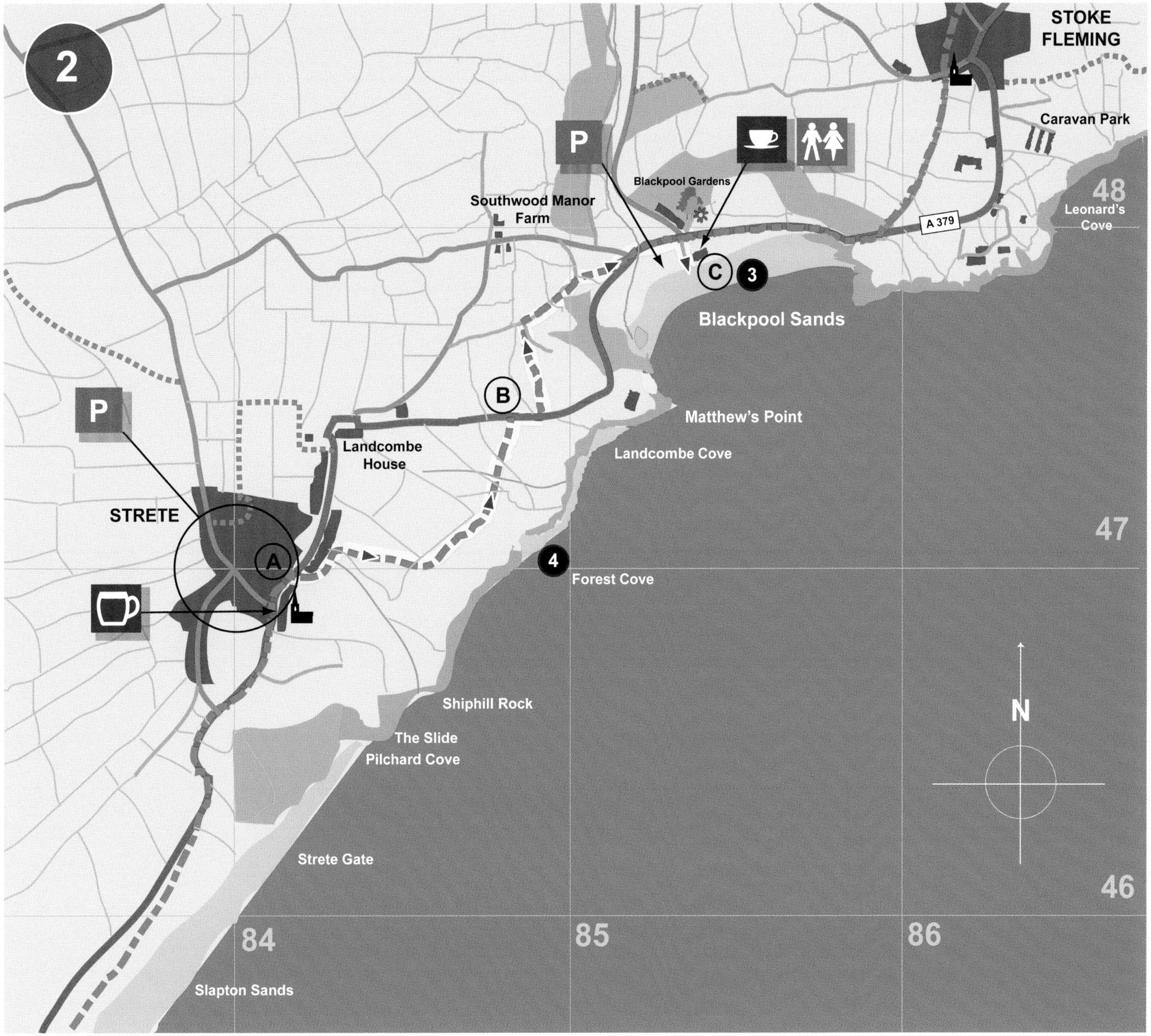

2
STOKE FLEMING
Caravan Park
P
Blackpool Gardens
Southwood Manor Farm
A 379
48
Leonard's Cove
C
3
Blackpool Sands
B
P
Matthew's Point
Landcombe House
Landcombe Cove
STRETE
A
47
4
Forest Cove
N
Shiphill Rock
The Slide
Pilchard Cove
Strete Gate
46
84
85
86
Slapton Sands



You now enter a narrow country lane and after a short distance look out for a stile over the hedgerow into the field on the right. Blackpool Sands can be seen from the crest of the hill and you wend your way down the well worn path to the bottom of the field. Cross a road and then a bridge over the brook that flows onto the beach, before re-crossing the A379 to Blackpool Sands. **(C)**

▲ **Leonard's Cove**

This stretch of coastline between Warren Point and Blackpool Sands is only approachable from the sea. Private farmland, clifftop properties and a caravan park preclude any clifftop walking.

# 2 STRETE TO NORTH HALLSANDS

▲ **Glorious June – Start Bay**

Walking west from Strete, the South West Coast Path drops steeply down to Strete Gate at the north end of Slapton Sands. The long sweep of Start Bay curves away to Start Point in the distance with the freshwater lake of Slapton Ley lying inside the shingle ridge.

## THE COASTLINE

The Queens Arms and Tower - Slapton

The long curve of Start Bay is a series of shingle beaches interrupted by Torcross Point, the headland that separates Torcross from Beesands, and Tinsey Head between Beesands and North Hallsands. Although all of the beaches in the Bay are called Sands they are in fact flint and quartz shingle thrown up and compressed by the sea to form a high, steep barrier that has entrapped the water catchments from the wooded hills. This has formed the two shallow freshwater lakes of Slapton Ley and Widdicombe Ley that flood the low lying land behind the shingle ridges.

The South West Coast Path hugs the shoreline for the full length of Start Bay, running along the shingle ridge of Slapton Sands, the promenades at Torcross and Beesands, and over the intervening hilltops and cliffs.

The picturesque and unspoilt villages of Slapton and Stokenham, nestled in the hills, display much of the traditional character of Devon hamlets with a cluster of attractive thatched and slate roofed cottages grouped around a church in cramped narrow lanes. The church at Stokenham is impressive with a striking stone built square tower, and although the church at Slapton is smaller it is beautifully proportioned. Both of these villages have excellent pubs with good cuisine.

The bare ridges of the surrounding hills are a patchwork of cultivated fields and the valleys are thickly wooded and criss-crossed with narrow, sunken lanes and footpaths that are a picture of colour in springtime when their high banks are in full bloom with wild flowers.

Only one thing mars this idyllic setting and that is its tenuous existence, precariously balanced under threat of erosion. In winter, when easterly gales coincide with high spring tides, the heavy seas can hammer and breach the shingle barrier causing sea water to spill into Slapton Ley upsetting its delicate ecology. For good reason sturdy curved sea wall defences protect the waterfront houses of Torcross and Beesands, reinforced by rip-rap boulders piled high against these bulwarks. The level of all beaches in Start Bay is continuously dropping, heightening the risk of storm damage.

The A379 coastal road linking Dartmouth to Kingsbridge, constructed on the natural crest of the shingle ridge, was partly swept away during a storm in January 2001 which raised questions and heated debate as to the viability, in both economic and environmental terms, of continuing to defend the road and the beach at Slapton Sands against further erosion and let nature take its course. The constant threat to this beautiful but fragile environment is blamed on the large scale dredging of shingle from the offshore Skerries Bank from 1897 to 1902, used in the construction of the Devonport dockyards in Plymouth. This regrettable rape of the seabed not only destroyed part of the natural protection of Start Bay against storm action but effectively removed materials that for centuries had constantly replenished and maintained beach levels.

## ACCESSIBLE BEACHES AND COVES

### Slapton Sands

Slapton Sands beach is 3¼ miles long from Pilchard Cove at its northern end to Torcross Point to the south. The beach can best be enjoyed at three locations; Strete Gate, Slapton Bridge and Torcross where there are public toilets and adequate car parking.

Dogs are allowed on Slapton Sands.

#### 1. Strete Gate

(Access Level 1)

This access to the beach is located at the bottom of the hill on the A379 below Strete, where there is a pay-and-display car park for 100 cars, public toilets and a picnic area. Steps drop down to the shingle beach that has a wide, level foreshore covered in a variety of flowering plants. From the ridge where the shingle is banked up high by the waves, the beach slopes steeply into the water and although swimming here is generally safe there can be a nasty undertow when there is strong wave action. Children will very quickly get out of their depth and should be competent swimmers or have constant supervision.

To the left of the car park the cliffs behind the beach rise up and at the far end they curve out to a headland that forms Pilchard Cove. Access to this cove is partially blocked by a landslip. 300 yards from the car park at the back of the beach are the remains of winding gear for winching up boats. From here to Pilchard Cove in the far corner is a naturist beach.

**Beesands**

#### 2. Slapton Bridge.

(Access Level 1)

There is a large pay-and-display car park for 360 cars in the middle of Slapton Sands at Slapton Bridge. This is at the junction of the A379 and the road to Slapton Village, clearly marked by the American war monument flanked by two flagpoles.

The characteristics of the beach at Slapton Bridge are the same as at Strete Gate, with a steeply shelving beach running quickly into deep water. This is the most exposed area of the beach and has the strongest wave action. There is no shade or shelter and it catches the wind from all directions. On still, sunny days a beach umbrella is recommended.

There are public toilet facilities and in the summer months an ice cream van is often to be found in the car park. If you get tired of the beach take a walk around the wooded shores of Slapton Ley, just a short stroll across Slapton Bridge.

#### 3. Torcross.

(Access Level 1)

The village straddles a small strip of land between the beach and Slapton Ley, with

**I can sing a rainbow – Torcross** ▲

The brightly coloured houses on the seafront at Torcross extend along the narrow strip of land between the beach of Slapton Sands and the shore of Slapton Ley. The village was evacuated during World War II when the area was used for military exercises in advance of the D-Day Normandy landings.

houses ranging up the hillside of Torcross Point and spreading a few hundred yards along the road to Stokenham. It is geared up for tourism but still retains the old world charm of a sea side resort with restaurants, cafés and pubs arranged on the short promenade.

Away from the beach there is a post office and general store, souvenir shop, a butcher's shop and a pottery. Seats are arranged around a clearing on the shores of Slapton Ley, popular with visitors who like to watch and hand feed the swans, geese and ducks that congregate there in numbers.

150 cars can be accommodated in the pay-and-display car parks and there are monuments to the WWII D-Day Landings sited in the corner of the main car park that include a Sherman Tank.

RNLI lifeguards patrol the beach during July and August and although swimming is generally safe, the same warning about undertow applies here as with the other locations on Slapton Sands.

There is a second small beach at Torcross that lies between Torcross Point and Limpet Rocks, accessible by a private road, but the beach can also be reached by walking along the shore below Torcross Point at low tide. This shingle beach is scoured by a fast flowing stream that cascades down one side and carves a deep gully across the shingle.

Torcross has been subjected to some horrendous storms in its history and in January 1979 huge waves crashed over the rooftops, heaving up stones and boulders from the beach, wrecking the waterfront properties. It was after this disaster that the curved sea wall and pilings were constructed.

**U.S. Army Memorial - Slapton Bridge**

**Sherman Tank Memorial**

**D-Day Landings Practice Area**

Due to similarities in the character of the beach and local terrain to those targeted in Normandy for the D-Day landings, Start Bay and in particular Slapton Sands was selected as the site for training exercises during WWII. The plan was to provide a realistic rehearsal for 'Operation Overlord' that was to spearhead the liberation of France.

The then Lord Lieutenant of Devon, Lord Fortescue, requisitioned the homes and lands of the villages of Blackawton, Chillington, East Allington, Sherford, Slapton, Stokenham, Strete and Torcross together with many outlying farms, and once these villages were evacuated, 15,000 American troops were billeted here to take part in the manoeuvres.

The training culminated in 'Exercise Tiger' held on the 27th and 28th April 1944 that through misfortune or incompetence or a combination of both, ended with the tragic loss of 749 U.S. servicemen. In the early hours of the 28th April after the successful landings of the fighting forces on the beach throughout the previous day; supporting troops and heavy equipment awaited their orders on board 8 Landing Ship Tanks lying in Lyme Bay. These were large flat bottom boats carrying hundreds of soldiers, trucks, jeeps and tanks. This fleet was intercepted by German E-boats patrolling the English Channel from their base in Cherbourg: fast moving motor torpedo boats that caused havoc and carnage by sinking two LST's and badly damaging a third.

Monuments to those soldiers and sailors that perished on that fateful night are to be found adjacent to the car park in Torcross. One of these is a 35ton Sherman Tank recovered from the seabed.

At Slapton Bridge there stands a memorial presented by the United States Army Authorities "...to the people of the South Hams who generously left their homes and their lands to provide a battle practice area for the successful assault in Normandy in June 1944."

Feeding Swans at Torcross

**4. Beesands**

(Access Level 1)

Beesands has a 1 mile long shingle barrier beach that links Dun Point and Tinsey Head in a straight line. The northern half of the beach is backed by a wide, flat area of grass that includes the village green and a children's playground. A rough gravel track runs along the back of the beach to the houses at Sunnydale that are tucked under Dun Point, and the freshwater lake of Widdecombe Ley fills the basin of the shallow valley leading up to Lower Widdecombe and Beeson.

The village of Beesands lines the waterfront of the southern half of the beach, the backs of the houses hard against the shoulder of the steep hill that rises to 300 feet at Huccombe Barn Cross. The houses are protected by a high curved sea wall and limestone rip-rap boulders are piled high against this wall and extend over the full length of the beach. The storm that hit Torcross in January 1979 also threatened to engulf this community and with the memories of the destruction of the village of South Hallsands in 1917 the sea defences were reinforced. As with Slapton Sands this beach level is continually sinking increasing the dangers of storm damage and today even more reinforcements are planned.

Two flights of wooden steps give access to the beach through breaks in the sea wall and there is a slipway for launching boats by the car park where the road to Beesands enters the village. The only means of getting to the north section of the beach is to clamber down over the rip-rap or walk along the shingle from the slipway.

In the early 19th century this was a thriving fishing community famous for its crabs that were sent up to Billingsgate market in London each week. Brittania Shellfish continues this proud tradition, a family run business with premises on the beach where visitors can buy fresh wet fish and shellfish or select a crab or lobster to be cooked on the spot to order.

The Cricket Inn is a cheerful pub that offers good food and sustenance and the souls of the residents are taken care of at the tiny St Andrew's Chapel.

The car park can hold 200 cars and there are public toilets.

Dogs are allowed on the beach.

**5. North Hallsands**

(Access Level 1)

North Hallsands is in the throes of a facelift. The Hallsands Hotel that once dominated this small cove was demolished in December 2006 to be replaced by 5 new dwellings. A house behind where the hotel once stood remains standing only because it has been colonised by bats that are a protected species, otherwise this building would have surely also been razed to the ground. A row of terraced houses teetering on the cliff edge, on rock undermined by wave action, were recently sold at auction; the new owners are obviously content to enjoy the benefits of this precarious perch above the sea until the inevitable happens.

The eroding fine shingle beach is protected by rip-rap brought in by barge and dumped along the shore.

At the time of writing North Hallsands is ravaged by a building site but once the new houses are completed it will resume its attraction as a sheltered quiet beach. There is parking for about 40 cars but there are no facilities.

Dogs are allowed on the beach.

**SLAPTON LEY NATURE RESERVE**

Slapton Ley is a lake comprising the Higher Ley and Lower Ley divided at Slapton Bridge. The Higher Ley is fen with extensive reed beds and marshes and the Lower Ley is the largest expanse of open fresh water in the South West. The National Nature Reserve covers 200 hectares and includes the lake, marshes, surrounding woodlands and the shingle barrier ridge thrown up by the sea. The freshwater run off from the catchments form the shallow lake. The reserve is owned by the Whitley Wildlife Trust and managed and run by The Field Studies Council with its field centre in Slapton village.

The ecology or balance of nature in the reserve is very delicate. The flow of fresh water through the lake is dependant on rainfall, and good quality water is essential to sustain the rich variety of fishes, birds, insects, mammals and plants that flourish in this habitat. It can be upset by an overdose of nutrients from the farmlands on the surrounding hills and storm breaches of the shingle barrier that increase salinity.

Fish stocks include pike, perch, roach, rudd and eel, and it is the eels that are the principle food source for the otters that colonise the lakeside. The surrounding wetlands provide wonderful habitat for many different species of bird, the most notable being a large population of cetti's warblers. On any walk along the Slapton Ley nature trail you can expect to see swans, ducks, moorhens and coots, and with a sharp eye you may be treated to sightings of great crested grebes, warblers, purple heron, or marsh harriers. In

spring and summer the marshes are lit up by the flowers of the yellow iris and the banks of the shingle ridge are a jazz of colour from yellow horned poppy and the vivid blue of viper's bugloss.

**Slapton Ley National Nature Reserve** ▲

The freshwater lake of Slapton Ley is divided into the Higher and Lower Ley at Slapton Bridge. The Lower Ley is the largest natural freshwater lake in the South West. The nature reserve encompasses the lake, marshes, reed beds and surrounding woodlands that provide a diversity of habitat for numerous species of fishes, birds, mammals, insects and plants.

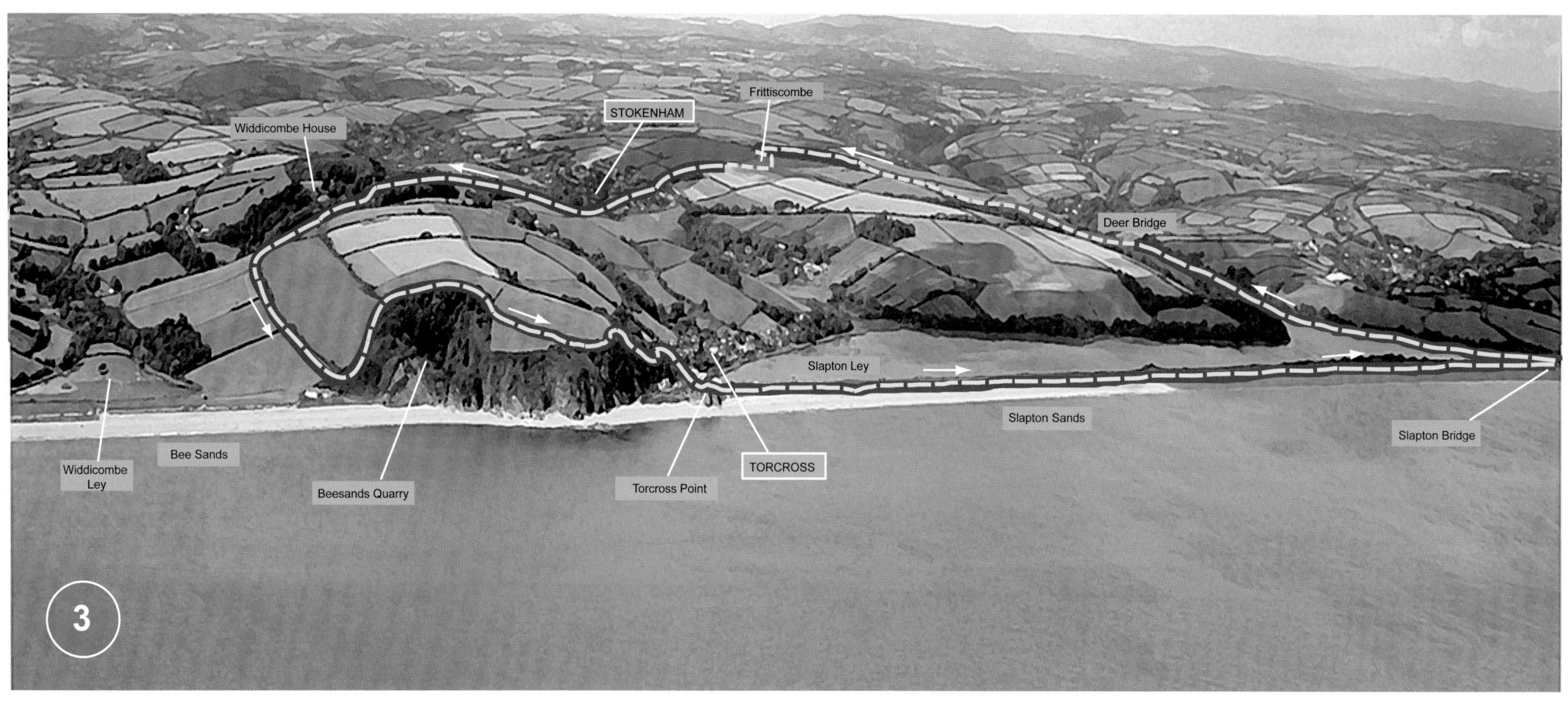


## WALK 3 SLAPTON LEY

**Distance** **6 miles**
**Time** **3¾ hours**
**Grade** **2**

The walk starts at the pay-and-display car park at Torcross. **(A)**

Don't forget your binoculars and the insect repellent!

Exit by the gate at the end of the car park and follow the footpath alongside Slapton Ley. After one mile you reach Slapton Bridge as the banks of the lake rise up and the path is separated from the water by a stand of small trees.

Cross the bridge on the road to Slapton village opposite the large car park and American war memorial. **(B)** The Higher Ley to the right of the bridge is a mass of dense reed beds with a channel of clear water down the middle that flows under the bridge into the open water of Slapton Ley. On the far side of the bridge is a private car park with a signpost to Deer Bridge 1 mile via the nature trail. Turn left through the gate.

A notice says "Otters and ground nesting birds, avoid disturbance. Dogs on a short lead please". There is a wooden decking with a board welcoming you to Slapton Ley National Nature Reserve with displays explaining the habitats and some of the wildlife you may encounter when walking the footpaths in the reserve. There is more information about Slapton Ley and bird identification in the small shelter beyond the kissing gate opposite the area of grass where white rowing boats are drawn up.

The footpath goes through a small copse along the shore of the lake with a high bank to the right. As you break through the trees the view opens out to the wide expanse of Slapton Ley with Torcross tucked away under the hills at the far end. This section of the nature trail used to have stiles at regular intervals but these have been removed making the walk much easier. There are flights of steps up and down but it is comfortable walking and not at all strenuous.

Moorhens and ducks paddle along the water's edge and you eventually come to a cantilevered platform with a seat and hand carved wooden panelling. This celebrates 60 years of the Slapton Ley Field Centre from

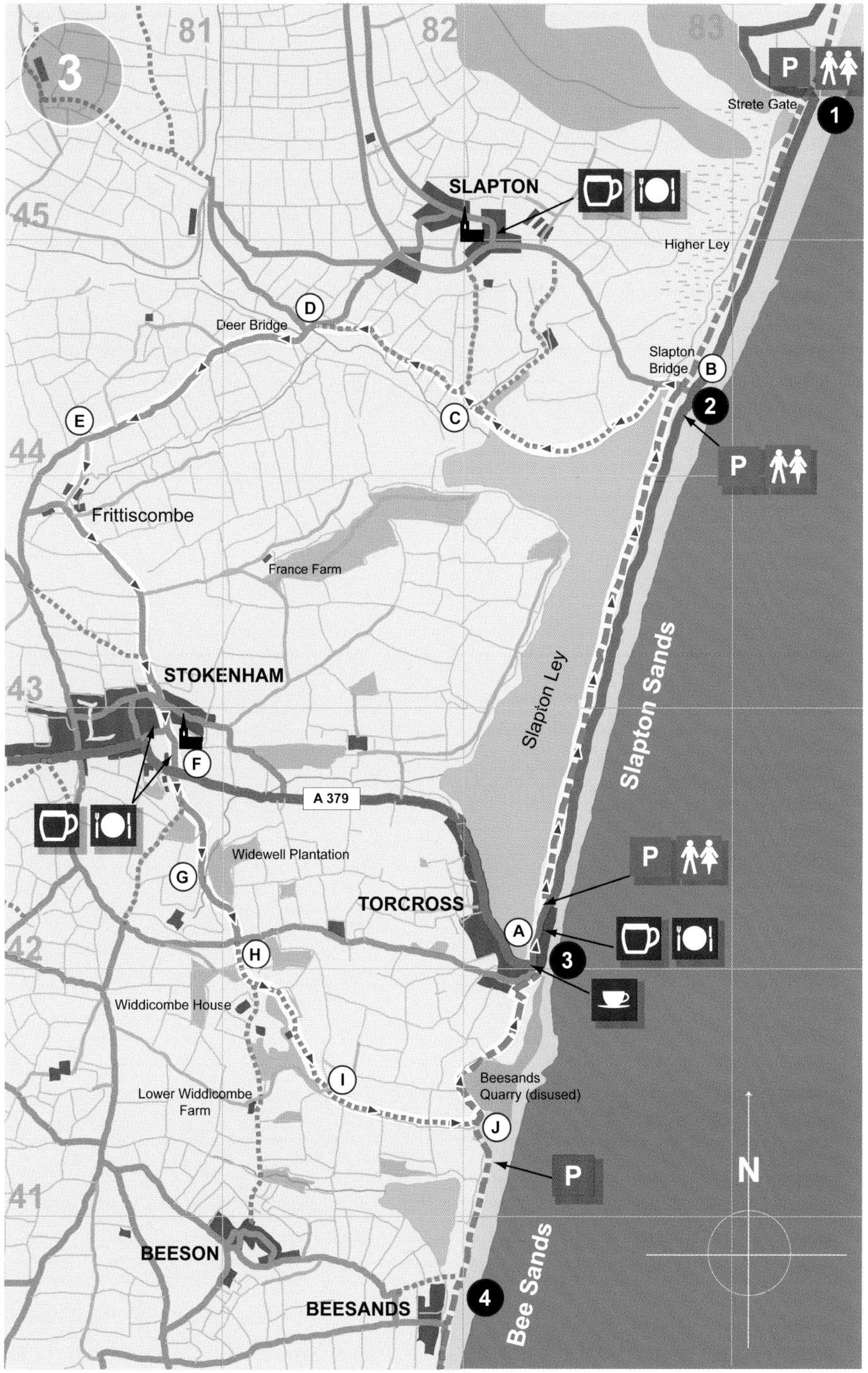

3

Strete Gate
SLAPTON
Higher Ley
Deer Bridge
Slapton Bridge
Frittiscombe
France Farm
STOKENHAM
A 379
Widewell Plantation
TORCROSS
Slapton Ley
Slapton Sands
Widdicombe House
Lower Widdicombe Farm
Beesands Quarry (disused)
BEESON
BEESANDS
Bee Sands
N

**Moorhens**

1943 to 2003, with the legend "FSC bringing environmental understanding to all". The carvings on the panels depict an assortment of insects, birds, otters and fishes.

Continue along the lakeside under a bower formed by a holly bush, after which the footpath swings away from the lake skirting wide marshland to the left with extensive thick reed beds. In springtime the yellow irises growing in the bog at the side of the path are in full bloom and the branches of fallen trees are reflected perfectly in the still water. You pass a five bar gate to the left at the entrance to a track that runs out to the middle of the marsh. A notice declares this as a sanctuary area.

After climbing up and over a small rise the footpath widens to a farm track leading up to a farm gate and a stile. **(C)** Follow the permissive route to Slapton Village ¼ mile to the left. This is a raised decking path with a sturdy handrail that crosses the marsh through trees covered in moss and lichens. At the end of this raised walkway take the footpath to Deer Bridge ¼ mile. This brings you to another wooden decked platform with seating and display boards that explain the ecology of the marshlands of the reserve. The colourful illustrated panels describe the diversity of life hidden underneath the water and the secretive life of the otter that breeds around the Ley, relying on eels for their main source of food. Also mentioned are the environmental protection initiatives like the Slapton Cyclo Project, Farm Stewardship Schemes and Community Awareness Programmes that help to manage Slapton Ley and the catchments that feed water into it.

Beyond this platform the aptly named Marsh Lane becomes a quagmire in winter and after prolonged periods of rain the water filled furrows can be very deep and slippery. Having negotiated this section of track you come out to the lane at Deer Bridge. **(D)**

Turn left over the bridge and start the steady climb up the sunken lane between high banks that in springtime are covered in primroses. At the crest of the hill is a farm gate on the left with views across to Slapton Village and the sea.

Turn left into Scrubs Lane to Frittiscombe ¼ mile. **(E)** Go down the hill turning right at the bottom passing some dilapidated barns and the farmyard on the left and then walk further out between high stone walls to the road.

Turn left, taking the lane that climbs steeply out of Frittiscombe over the hill to Stokenham. It bears right at the entrance to France Farm and then goes downhill passing an ivy clad ruin to a T-junction in the village.

Turn right and then immediately left down a narrow lane between high banks and stone walling that comes out at the side of The Tradesman's Arms, where you turn left again towards the church and on down past The Church House Inn to the A379.

**Stokenham**

Cross the main road into the lane opposite, next to Stokenham House. **(F)** Pass The Vicarage and then Riddlesfoot Lane on the right and continue straight on. This is a really pretty country lane and looking back there is a nice view of Stokenham across the valley with its impressive church and the line of white, thatched cottages arranged on the hill facing the village green. Down the valley towards the sea you catch glimpses of Slapton Ley.

The woods covering the top of the hill directly ahead is Widewell Plantation and there are paths through the plantation that can be taken as an alternative to the lane. (A couple of railway sleepers bridge a small stream and steps go up the bank to a stile. **(G)** Once in the plantation be sure you take the footpath that returns to the lane further up.) The lane comes out to a T-junction. **(H)**

A post box is set into a stone wall and a metal gate gives entry to the field opposite signposted as a footpath to Beeson 1 mile. Go straight up the grass bank to the top of the field where you will find a second metal gate opening into the grounds of Widdicombe House. Turn left down the driveway past ornamental gardens and mature trees that screen the blue slate roofs of the mansion. At the entrance to the house, flanked by stone walls, take the gravel driveway to cottages off to the left. A footpath goes around the cottages and carries on down through the woods and over a stile into a lane. **(I)** From here you can see the north end of Beesands beach, the freshwater lake of Widdicombe Ley and the village of Beeson on the hillside to your right.

Cross the lane, climb over the second stile and head down to the lower hedgerow of this sloping field. The footpath keeps to the hedge and farm gates give views out to Start Point and the lighthouse. At the bottom of the field you come to another stile and the coastal path. Turn left in the direction of Torcross ½ mile. **(J)**

The coast path climbs steeply up and around the derelict Beesands Quarry. At places steps are cut into the hillside to help the climb. On the right you see the ravine where the blue slate was hewn from the cliff face; where tall trees now grow from the base of this old excavation. A gap in the fence on

the left allows you to look back down the valley to Widdicombe Ley, along the length of Beesands beach and the high cliffs of Start Point. In winter the smoking chimneys of Beesands and Beeson send light streamers across the darkened hillsides.

At the top of the hill the path continues around the back of the quarry coming to a farm gate and a grass field overlooking Start Bay to the north. Through the gate a line of telegraph poles trace the direction of the path down the field to Torcross. As you round the corner you are looking straight along the length of Slapton Sands. The village on the top of the hill in the distance is Strete and the small village to the left in the middle of the hillside is Slapton. The footpath, clearly indicated by waymarkers, jinks left and right on its way down to the village.

If you take the last section of the path to the right at Cliff House you get a splendid view of Torcross and a flight of stone steps curve down under an arch to bring you out to the promenade.

▲ **Summer Haze - Slapton Ley**

The high shingle barrier ridge of Slapton Sands is carpeted with a rich variety of plants that include sea radish, yellow horned poppy and vipers bugloss. In spring and summer the coastal path that runs the full length of the Lower Ley shimmers in a blaze of colour.

Widdicombe House
BEESON
Higher Middlecombe Farm
Widdicombe Ley
BEESANDS
Tinsey Head
BICKERTON
North Hallsands
Hall Sands
START BAY
4

## WALK 4 BEESANDS

| | |
|---|---|
| **Distance** | **4½ miles** |
| **Time** | **2½ hours** |
| **Grade** | **2** |

The walk starts at the free car park in Beesands. **(A)**

Walk across the village green past the fresh water lake of Widdicombe Ley and on to the houses at Sunnydale at the far end of the beach. The coastal footpath passes around the back of the white house and 30 yards beyond there is a footpath to the left signposted to Widewell 1 mile. **(B)**

Step over the stile and take the path up the valley keeping to the left-hand hedgerow of this steeply sloping field. This part of the walk retraces a short section of Walk 3. Climbing to the top of the field you pass gateways in the hedgerow that open up views to Start Point and the lighthouse, as well as Widdicombe Ley and the waterfront at Beesands. From the first gate the path widens out to a farm track.

**Beesands Quarry**

Sunnydale is a disused stone quarry, its derelict workings carved deep into the cliff face at Dun Point, the headland separating Torcross and Beesands. In the 18th century blue slate was extracted, split and squared and transported out to the shore on rails, where it was then loaded into boats. The entrance to the quarry can be reached at low water from Beesands' beach but due to beach erosion it now stands 10 feet above the shingle. Apart from the scar left by the excavation, nothing remains of the steam engine and equipment that was used to process and handle the slate. All that is left is a ladder to the cliff top probably used by the workers to access the quarry during high water.

At the top of the field climb over the stile and step across the lane to the next stile. **(C)** (Unfortunately the lane to Lower Widdicombe Farm to the left of the stile is not a public right of way and to reach the farm it is necessary to take this detour around the perimeter of the grounds of Widdicombe House.) Walk up the footpath at the edge of the copse. The left hand bank drops into a dell and the sides are covered in rhododendrons and mature beech trees.

The path passes to the right of two cottages and out to their gravel driveway that merges with the road at the entrance to the manor. Further along the road a footpath signposted to Beeson **(D)** runs downhill through woodland passing at the back of Widdicombe House to meet the lane at Lower Widdecombe Farm. You pass through a five bar gate at the bottom of the field and the footpath to Beeson is directly opposite past the farm. The public footpath signpost

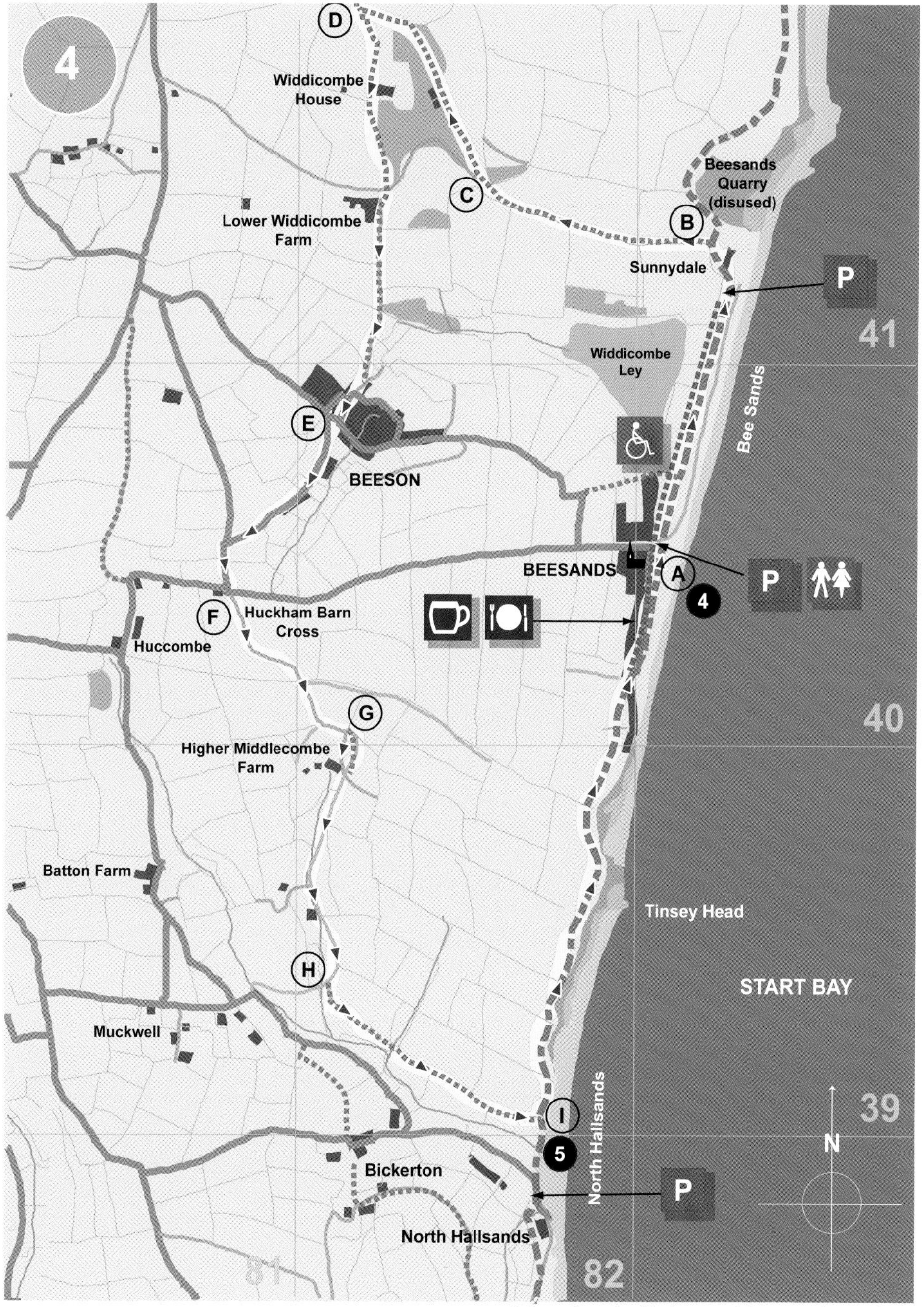

**North Hallsands** ►

Hallsands is a fine shingle beach sheltered from prevailing westerly winds by Start Point. This painting was created from studies made in 1998. Since that time the Hallsands Hotel has been boarded up and then demolished. The new houses being built on this site will change the character of this quiet cove.

◄ **Tidying up – Lower Widdicombe**

The old world charm of living in a beautiful, rustic, thatched Devon cottage in peaceful and idyllic surroundings can loose its edge as backache sets in during a clearing up session in the garden.

MILES 2005

is on the left next to an old barn faced with rough timbers and a corrugated roof.

There are two five bar gates mounted side by side and it is the right-hand gate that opens into a lovely sunken lane completely overdecked by branches. The footpath crosses the stream that feeds Widdicombe Ley and eventually, upon entering Beeson, the sunken path opens out into a gravel track beyond the playing field. At the road turn right and walk up to the T-junction and then left down into the middle of the village. This is a quiet hamlet with neither pub nor church, just a group of attractive houses.

As the road turns sharp left take the lane to the right up the hill past the telephone booth and post box. **(E)** This is a long steady climb and a second lane merges from the right. You continue up the hill passing a complex of tastefully converted barns until you reach the T- junction where you turn left. After 70 yards you come to Huccombe Barn Cross and no one will need to tell you that this is 300 feet above the car park at Beesands. **(F)** One consolation is that it is practically all down hill from here to North Hallsands.

Take the road signed "Farm Only" and as you top the rise Start Point Lighthouse comes back into view

At the private entrance to Higher Middlecombe Farm there is a footpath to the left of the gates to Muckwell that skirts around the farm. **(G)** The footpath comes out to a five bar gate with the farm on your right. Pass through the gate and turn left down to a second five bar gate that opens out into a farm track. Looking back, the farm stands high among the trees above an old overgrown orchard that spreads down the hillside. This wider track is flanked by stone walls and as you walk down the valley the masts on the top of Start Point can be seen. Pass through the next gate with a red arrow on the left-hand post and continue along this secluded quiet track. A stream runs down the side which will provide welcome refreshment for a thirsty dog. As the path levels out there is a signpost with a green arrow pointing to the left to Hallsands. **(H)**

You pass through a swing gate onto National Trust land and a grass track to a small field. A stream flows along the right-hand side opening out to a pond. At the end of the field take the path bearing off to the right signposted to "Beesands Via Coast Hallsands". There are stepping stones over a small brook and the path continues along the left-hand hedgerow. The hedgerows here are matted with high brambles and in late August and early September the bushes are laden with blackberries.

A gate opens into a sunken track with high banks on either side that brings you to yet another gate opening to a field. The path crosses the field to the beach at North Hallsands. **(I)** (With the demolition of the Hallsands Hotel in December 2006 and the planning approval for building 5 new houses, Hallsands will be a building site during 2007 after which it will hopefully return to its former tranquillity.)

The coastal path back to Beesands keeps to the natural contours above the grass topped cliffs of Tinsey Head. At low tide a wide shingle beach spreads out from the foot of the cliffs but this foreshore is only accessible for a stroll at low spring tides. The path goes through several gates separating fields where sheep graze for most of the year, so keep the dog on the lead.

**Barn at Lower Widdicombe Farm**

From Tinsey Head you can see the whole expanse of Start Bay from the lighthouse on the tip of Start Point to the Mew Stone beyond the mouth of the River Dart. Rounding the headland the beach at Beesands runs away below in a straight line.

At the split in the path take the right-hand fork to Beesands and an amble along the promenade past the Cricket Inn brings you back to the car park.

# 3 SOUTH HALLSANDS TO EAST PRAWLE

**Start Point Lighthouse** ▲

Start Point is one of the most prominent landmarks on the South Hams coast. Strong rip currents race around this rugged peninsula that has laid claim to many lives as ships foundered and sank on its rocks and shoals. The lighthouse has stood on its lofty perch since 1836.

## THE COASTLINE

The most dramatic feature of this stretch of the coast is Start Point with its high jagged cliffs of green and mica schist surmounted by the prominent, white-painted Start Point Lighthouse. This imposing headland stretching out eastwards as a long tail into the English Channel marks the southern end of Start Bay. "Start" was Anglo-Saxon for tail; hence the name.

The final curve of Start Bay from South Hallsands to Froweder Point below the lighthouse has 150 ft cliffs with deep ravines that drop down vertically into the sea. There are no accessible beaches or coves and the foreshore is littered with large boulders from old rock falls. The beach below the ruined village of South Hallsands has been cut off by a landslide and is considered too dangerous for public access. The steeply sloping gorse and bracken covered hillsides rise up to 360 feet topped by the tall masts of the Start Point radio transmitting station.

This is a treacherous place for shipping. Strong tidal currents constantly race and eddy around Start Point, and many ships have been lost in these waters. Navigators did not have the comfort and security of the lighthouse beacon or the fog siren unti 1836.

The cliffs and steep hillsides south of the lighthouse run westward rounding the heel of the promontory at Great Sleadon Rock and then opening out to the gentler slopes of Lannacombe Bay. A long grass valley leads down from the car park at Start Farm to Great Mattiscombe Sand. The coastal path that until now ran high up the bracken covered hillsides around Start Point, drops down to wend its way across a plateau of narrow grass fields at the edge of low, crumbling cliffs above the shoreline. Pinnacles of shale are left exposed by erosion at the back of wide platforms of rock.

Lannacombe Beach lies at the head of a lushly wooded valley irrigated by a stream. The small lane along the valley floor to Lannacombe Cottage offers the only car access to this section of the coast, the next opportunity being the lane from East Prawle winding out to Prawle Point.

The shoreline of Lannacombe Bay is characterized by Ballsaddle Rock at the foot of Woodcombe Point and Gorah Rocks further along by Malcombe Point, where very wide, rock bedding planes with sea-washed gullies, deep crevasses and rock pools fan out into the sea. An escarpment rises away from the low sea cliffs to a high ridge with exposed rock tors and it is not until after Woodcombe Point that the hills begin to slope away more gently, with broad grass fields at their base. Lannacombe Bay is beautiful, wild and remote.

**The Pinnacles**

**Start Point Transmitting Station**

The masts and aerials on the top of Start Point are part of a broadcasting station that currently transmits BBC Radio Five Live on 693 kHz. It first came on air in 1939 to broadcast the West of England Regional Programme. During the war it sent out the Forces Programme and at various periods of time The Home Service, Radio 4 and Radio 1 were broadcast from this transmitter.

**Winter Sunset – Lannacombe Bay** ▲

Lannacombe Bay lies between Start Point and Prawle Point and is one of the least accessible stretches of the South Hams coast with very restricted car parking close to the shore. A high escarpment rises sharply above low cliffs that surmount a solid barricade of wide flat rock ledges. These ledges take the brunt of the sea's advances.

**South Hallsands circa: 1900** ▲

This painting has been created from archive photographs of the doomed fishing village of South Hallsands built somewhat precariously on rock ledges above a steeply banked shingle beach in Start Bay. Now only skeletal ruins bear witness to its existence, the houses having been swept from their foundations during a violent storm on January 26th 1917.

## SOUTH HALLSANDS

It seems remarkable that the village of South Hallsands built upon exposed rock ledges and huddled low under high cliffs within sight of Start Point should have withstood the ravages of storms for almost 200 years. The fishermen and their families that established this hamlet and managed to eke out a meagre living fishing the waters of Start Bay, must have had full confidence in the durability and safety of their homesteads, borne out by their survival for over two centuries.

It was a harsh environment and perilous work in which women were also involved in the physical toil of launching and landing boats on a steeply shelving, stone and shingle beach in all weathers and sea conditions. It is said that wives carried their menfolk into the boats on occasions to keep them dry before they rowed out to the fishing grounds. This close community brought up their children, worshipped in their chapel, supported one another and struggled against hardship, illness and poverty on those narrow rock ledges, until fate took a hand in the shape of an Admiralty contract to expand the naval dockyards in Plymouth in 1896.

The construction work required vast amounts of concrete and the building contractor was granted permission by the Government to dredge ballast from shingle banks off the coast of Start Bay. Despite deputations by the villagers through their M.P., voicing their concerns that this dredging would be detrimental to the fishing grounds and threaten their livelihoods, 600,000 tons of shingle was dredged from the sea bed.

As a result the beach level began to fall and sea walls became damaged as waves regularly crashed against them during high spring tides. Some houses were lost and a new sea wall was built but the erosion of the beach continued until it reached a level where fishing boats could no longer be safely moored without risk of them being dashed against the rocks.

On the night of January 26th 1917, high tides and gale force winds blowing from the southeast coincided to breach the sea wall defences and sweep away four houses. The village was evacuated and records show that fortunately nobody was killed or seriously injured. Villagers watched dismayed from the clifftops as the storm raged throughout the night and the following day. More houses collapsed as the sea smashed through doors and windows surging backwards and forwards until the walls gave way leaving forlorn gables standing sentinel above the rubble.

Amazingly some of these gables and stub walls remain standing today as a sad monument and stark reminder of the consequences of such wanton destruction of the environment.

**The ruins of South Hallsands**

## ACCESSIBLE BEACHES AND COVES

### 1. Great Mattiscombe Sand.

(Access Level 3)

This beach is remotely located at the east end of Lannacombe Bay under the lee of Start Point. A footpath from the Start Point car park leads down a long grass valley, often with grazing cattle, following the course of a brook that eventually tumbles down the rock face onto the beach. The South West Coast Path skirts along the low cliffs at the back of the beach and a steep, narrow track zigzags down the cliff face in the corner of the cove at the point where the footpath and the coastal path meet.

The beach is coarse sand backed by recessed rock ledges that provide secluded places for sunbathing. At high tide a wide area of sandy beach remains in the corner by the track. There is good bathing but care should be taken when there is a strong swell and high waves are driven in from the south west. A wide expanse of sand is exposed at low water and Mattiscombe Rock thrusts high out of the sand at the far end of the beach, its base carved away by wave action. Beyond are rock ledges that project into the sea at the back of which stand unique pinnacles sculpted by erosion.

On quiet days seals are often seen off the beach, particularly in the waters surrounding Great Sleaden Rock.

There are no facilities.

Lannacombe Beach

## 2. Lannacombe Beach.

(Access Level 1)

Lannacombe Beach can be approached by car from South Allington or Kellaton. At the road junction at Lannacombe Green, a narrow lane to Lannacombe Beach is signposted. This runs down to the seashore along a beautiful, secluded, wooded valley. Parking is limited to approximately 12 cars at the back of the sea wall. It is first-come-first-served and if the parking area is full then there is nothing for it but to spend the day somewhere else. To reach the beach from the coastal path there is a 30 minute walk from the nearest car park at Start Point.

There is very little beach at high tide but this quickly widens out to a glorious expanse of sand as the tide recedes. Below the sea wall are rip-rap boulders but there is a slipway. Lannacombe Cottage is tucked into the corner of the cove by the side of a stream that runs through a culvert under the road and then courses down the rocks and flows and spreads out across the beach. The beach is flanked on either side by low cliffs and the left side is strewn with boulders and rock outcrops. Low tide offers great opportunities for rock pooling. Bathing is safe and the beach is sheltered from anything but a southerly wind.

Dogs are allowed.

There are no facilities

A few minutes walk westward, there is a path and slipway down to a small sandy beach immediately in front of what was originally a row of Coastguard cottages. This beach is recognisable by a winch and tackle and some upturned boats .

## 3. Woodcombe Sand.

(Access Level 3)

Woodcombe Sand is clearly signposted from the coastal path on the east side of Woodcombe Point. The beach nestles at the back of a deep, narrow ravine. From the coastal path a level grass track passes between thorn bushes and then drops into the back of this ravine. A stream flows down the valley and a footbridge crosses the cascade and a flight of steps descend to the beach of coarse sand and gravel. The middle of the beach is flat bedrock and shingle channels run out into the sea on either side. The stream gouges its way down the middle of the shingle and out across the flat bedrock. At the back of the beach low cliffs rise up covered in ivy, gorse and shrubs.

There is a corrugated asbestos building at the back of the beach that serves as a boathouse and a notice declares that it is a private beach. “Please respect its beauty and tranquillity”.

The beach does not appear to be an ideal place for swimming.

**Approaching Fog Bank – Start Point** ►

Start Point is at the end of a peninsula that projects one mile out to sea at the southern tip of Start Bay. It is one of the most exposed headlands on the south coast of England. Crab and lobster fishing in Start Bay had its heyday in the late 1800s but lines of pots are still laid out each day and succulent local caught fresh fish, shellfish and crabs are served at hotels, restaurants and pubs’ around Start Bay.

DH63
MILES 2005

## WALK 5 START POINT

**Distance** **4¾ miles**
**Time** **2¾ hours**
**Grade** **3**

From Stokenham follow the road to Beesands and Hallsands via Dunston Cross and Kellerton Cross, finally turning left to South Hallsands from the road out to Start Point.

The walk starts from the free car park at South Hallsands. **(A)**

The grass and gravel car park is to the right of the lane as it dips before climbing to Trout's Holiday Apartments on the cliff top. There is no parking beyond this point but there is a turning space by Trout's Servery.

Below Trout's Apartments the remains of the ruined village of South Hallsands can be viewed from a platform with display boards showing photographs and explaining the history of the disaster that struck in 1917. Because the cliffs are unstable there is no public access to the beach, the old right of way having been swept away by the sea.

The first part of the walk is a steady climb along the coast path to the car park on Start Point. A signpost gives this at 1¼ miles. The final curve of Start Bay out to the point is a buttress of vertical cliffs carved with deep clefts and ravines. The grass and bracken covered hillside rises steeply from the cliff edge to the crown of the peninsula. The footpath traverses the hillside and at places the branches of stubby trees, swept by the wind to the contour of the hillside, form tunnels and bowers. Just before you reach the car park the path gets a little steeper and steps have been cut out to arrest any further erosion.

Pass through a kissing gate into the car park. **(B)** This is a pay car park that can be used as an alternative starting point for this walk. It is not attended in the off-peak seasons.

Cross to the wide gate and stone stile at the entrance of the road to the lighthouse. A signpost points to a public footpath on the right to the beach of Great Mattiscombe Sand ½ mile. Directly ahead, in the direction of the walk, Lannacombe is given at a distance of 2½ miles. Climb the stile or open the gate and walk down the road to the lighthouse.

Looking back over the wall the whole of Start Bay out to the mouth of the River Dart and beyond is laid out before you, the bright shingle beaches of Hallsands, Beesands and Slapton Sands clearly visible. Here you get a different perspective of the ruined village but you will need binoculars to really appreciate it.

The road to the lighthouse is a dead end and the coastal path crosses over the skeletal spine of the headland just after a wooden hut to the right of the road. **(C)** Here an optimistic signpost states "Coast Path to Minehead 462 miles" and "Coast Path to Poole Dorset 168 miles". You will probably settle for the walk to Lannacombe and back!

The lighthouse ½ mile further on is well worth a visit. The schedule of public opening times and guided tours is not

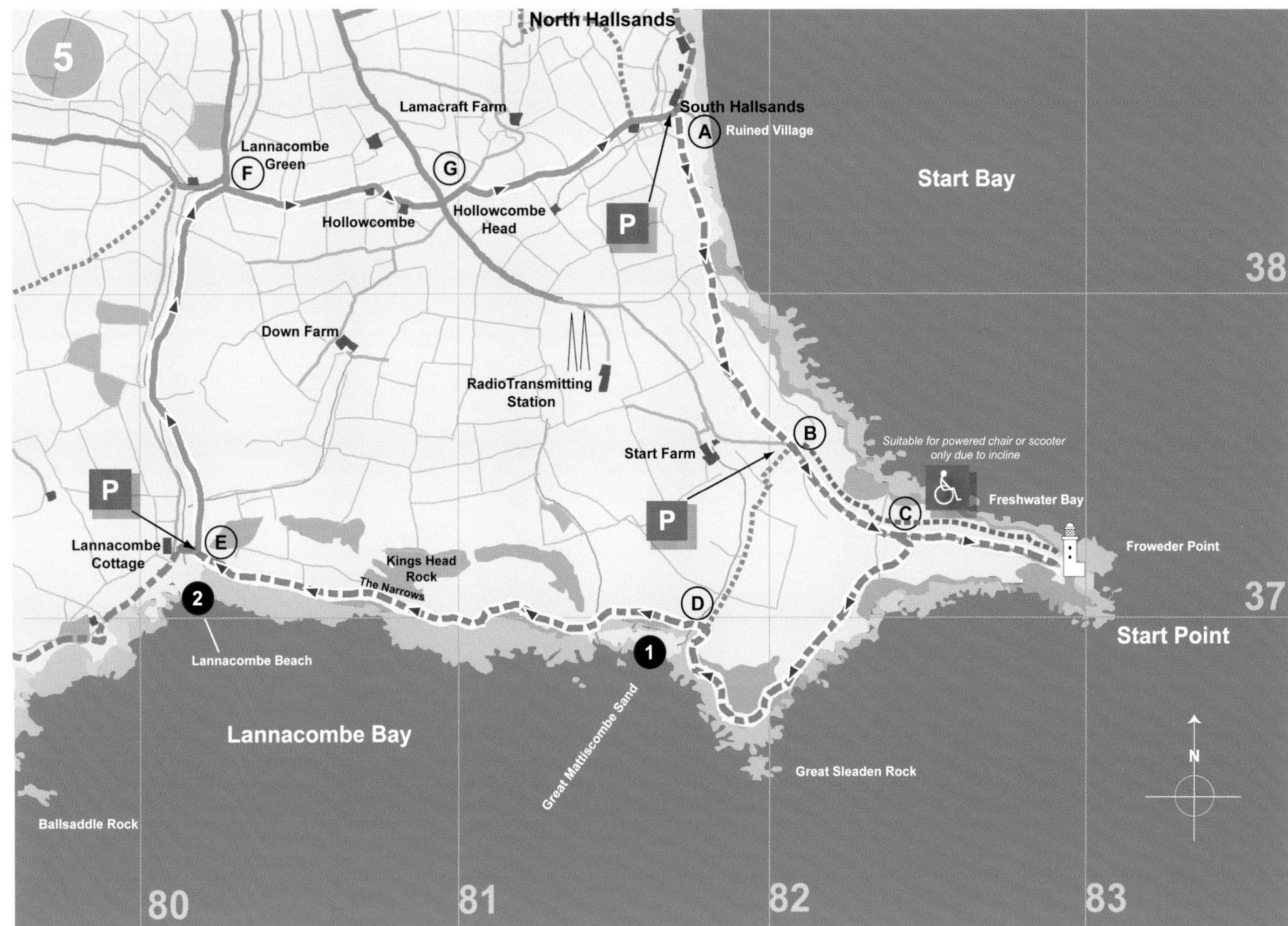



regular throughout the year but a pamphlet is available from the Tourist Information Office. It is best to check opening times when planning the day out if the lighthouse visit is to be a highlight of the walk.

Cross the ridge to the other side and turn right in the direction of the waymarkers. Note the sign that says "Use extreme care when using this section of the path". The path wends its way across the grass slope of the hillside but as it descends to the corner of the next headland and the huge slab of Great Sleadon Rock, it becomes very rough and rocky. There is a second worn path lower down the hillside running away from the lighthouse, the white tower at this point now visible from the southern side of the Point.

The coastal path, hewn out of the rock in places, rounds the next headland. This is a rough clamber and a good place to wrick your ankle if you are not careful. The path then flattens out where an area of grass slopes down to the low cliffs and Great Sleadon Rock. Rounding the corner Great Mattiscombe Sand comes into view. A signpost warns "Danger keep to coastal path" marked by yellow arrows and it is clear to see where the old path passed close to the cliff edge with tufted grass and hidden overhangs.

At Great Mattiscombe Sand the slope of the grass hillside lays as a carpet above low crumbling cliffs at the base of which a wide expanse of flat bedrock spreads out as a broad platform to the sandy beach. In the corner of the cove, where the stream tumbles down to the beach, a signpost shows the way back to the car park on Start Point ½ mile and westward to Lannacombe 1 mile. **(D)** Continue along the coast path that skirts along the back of the beach passing the pinnacles and across grass fields called The Narrows beneath the tor of Kings Head Rock. From here you can see the archway at the base of Prawle Point on the far side of the bay.

You cross a sparkling brook, pass through a gate and over yet another rivulet with stepping stones. The way opens out in wider pastures and although signs entreat hikers to keep to the coastal path along the cliff edge, the well worn track across the middle of the fields is proof that the majority of walkers do not heed the request. Stone markers and red tipped posts mark the boundaries along the cliff edge where they are most fragile.

It is a level easy stroll to Lannacombe Beach where the wide flat bedrock on the foreshore gives way to a beautiful sandy beach. **(E)** The coast path goes on to Prawle Point 2½ miles distant but it is here that you leave the shoreline and walk inland along the lane up the wooded valley away from the beach. This is a narrow road with few passing places so keep an eye and ear open for approaching cars. Although the parking at Lannacombe Beach is severely restricted there is a constant flow

Start Point Lighthouse

**Start Point Lighthouse**

For 150 years this lighthouse has guided shipping safely around Start Point. Its white beam that flashes 3 times every 10 seconds stands 203 feet above sea level and can be seen 25 miles out to sea. Not only does the lighthouse signal the position of Start Point to navigators but a static red light on the tower pinpoints the location of the Skerries Bank. When visibility threatens safe passage, a fog horn sends out its bass tone every 60 seconds until the mists clear.

When it was originally built in 1836 the mechanism for operating the revolving light was driven by a heavy weight that dropped vertically down a tube from a machine-room at the cliff face. In 1959 electricity was finally cabled to the light and the lighthouse became fully automated in 1993.

The lighthouse keeper's cottages are now let for holidays and the tower is open to the public with guided tours.

of traffic from ever optimistic motorists. (Note: This short stretch of the walk is shared with Walk 6.)

At the T-junction at Lannacombe Green **(F)**, turn right to start the long, steady climb up to the cross-roads at Hollowcombe Head. This is the most tiring part of the walk. Nearing the top you pass two white-painted cottages on a right-hand bend, followed by the farmhouse and converted barns of Hollowcombe.

Go straight over the cross-roads **(G)** signposted South Hallsands and after the entrance to Lamacraft Farm the high banked country lane runs thankfully downhill for ½ mile back to the car park.

## WALK 6 LANNACOMBE BAY

| **Distance** | **4¾ miles** |
|---|---|
| **Time** | **3 hours** |
| **Grade** | **3** |

The walk starts at East Prawle village green. **(A)**

Leave the village green along the no-through road that passes to the right of Grunter's Café and wends its way down towards the coast. Prawle Point comes into view as the road gets steeper and bends to the right. The footpath goes down the side of Bayfield, the last cottage of the row of houses on the left.

The path slopes gently downhill between high hedgerows. (Part way down the path, before you reach the T-junction, there is a stone stile set into the wall on the left. This is a short cut that crosses the corner of the field. The short cut is steep and slippery in wet conditions.) If you continue to the bottom of the hill you turn left and are treated to the first view of Lannacombe Bay with the wide rock ledges of Gorah Rocks in the foreground.

This wider stony track with a water gulley running down the left-hand side has high banks and hedges that frame the picture of the bay ahead. After bearing to the left the path gets steeper and more uneven.

Pass through a five bar gate into a field where the path splits on either side of a hedgerow that separates two fields and although the signpost indicates that the footpath is to the right of the hedge, the beaten track is on the left. At the far end of the field a signpost shows the way to Lannacombe 1½ miles and you have reached the coastal path. **(B)**

The path runs along the edge of fields above the line of low cliffs. The high escarpment of Hines Hill and The Torrs sweeps up from the fields on the left and continues unbroken to the rock outcrops above Woodcombe Point in the distance. This impressive ridge with a matt of trees and shrubs on its slopes makes this one of the more remote stretches of the South Hams coastline. At low tide the wide expanse of Gorah Rocks is exposed, the flat ledges interspersed with deep channels and covered in rock pools. Needless to say this

rocky foreshore is to be avoided when heavy seas are running.

A gate set in stone walling opens into the next field and dog owners should be alert to sheep that are often grazing here. The Edwardian mansion of Maelcombe House, with its distinctive red roof and timbered gables stands in its own grounds surrounded by pine trees. Once through the next gate the coastal path runs along the fence line of this property and in summer, white hydrangeas bloom under a canopy of trees.

After two more gates you leave the Maelcombe House Estate and enter an area of wilderness and the path reduces to a well worn, narrow track between high bracken. The path climbs up around the back of Stinking Cove eroded into the cliff face. At the highest point of the path you come to another gate after which it descends down rough hewn steps and worn rocks and stones. Keep a sharp look out for a herd of mountain goats that forage among the shrubs; they can often be seen on the hillside or on the lower slopes.

The path levels out as houses at Lannacombe come into view and the enormous flat slabs of Grant's Rock and Ballsaddle Rock rise up as platforms at the water's edge. Rounding the corner the path rises once again around another small cove and across the valley stands an attractive house with dormer windows and a wide conservatory. It has an idyllic location looking out to sea over a garden of lawned terraces ending in steps to the private beach of Woodcombe Sand. Once past the signpost to this beach the sea view disappears as you enter a copse of hawthorn bushes. You come to a gate and a notice asks politely, " Please shut all gates and stay on paths, thank you".

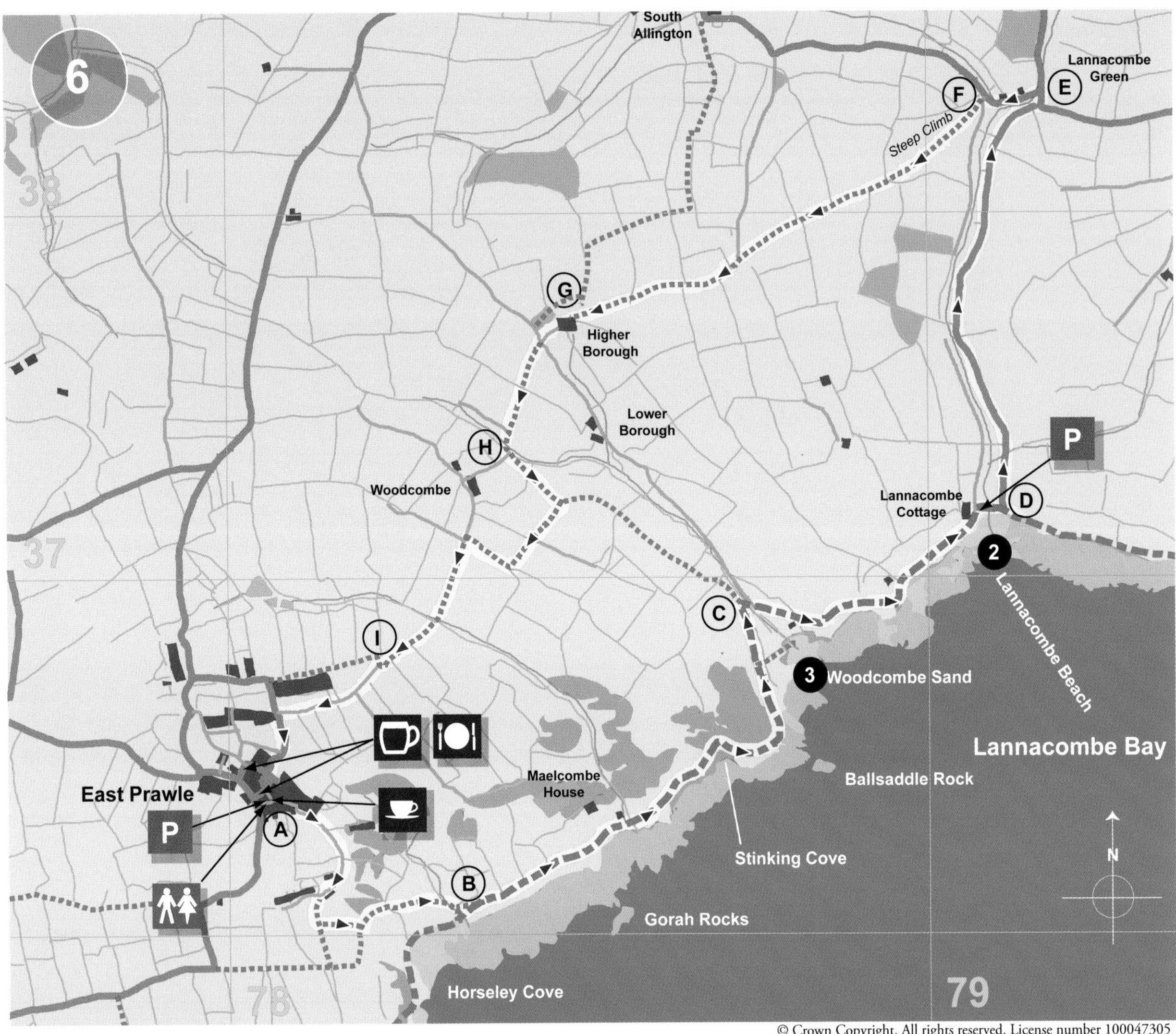




The path around the boundary of this estate is level and makes for easy walking.

Just before the house, the path splits, the track uphill signposted to Woodcombe ¾ mile. **(C)** (For those not wishing to do the full circuit via Lannacombe in order to avoid the strenuous climb at the head of the valley, this path can be used as a short cut back to East Prawle. It is a steady climb to the top but not half as challenging.)

The coastal path goes through a five bar gate, over a wooden bridge that crosses a stream and comes out at the driveway to the house. This road runs up the valley parallel with the footpath to Woodcombe but the way is barred and a notice declares "No Public Access".

From here the coast path out to Lannacombe widens out, passing through two five bar gates and runs alongside a house that was once Coastguard cottages. The path merges with the farm track to this house that leads on to Lannacombe Cottage and the beach. **(D)** Here the walk leaves the shore and heads inland along the lane up the wooded valley to Lannacombe Green. (Note: This short stretch of the walk is shared with Walk 5.) This is a narrow road with few passing places so keep an eye and ear open for approaching cars.

At the T-junction **(E)** you turn left and immediately left again on the road to South Allington and Chivelstone. The road bends sharply right at a group of houses, a mill and a stream and starts to climb. Just past the bend there is a signpost on the left for the footpath/bridleway to East Prawle. A five bar gate opens to the bridleway; pass through the gate but take the footpath up the bank through the copse immediately on the right. **(F)** If you make a mistake and miss the footpath, the bridleway has fallen into disuse and you will soon walk into a tangle of brambles and stinging nettles.

Once you have cleared the tree line and walked up through the bracken, the most arduous part of the walk begins. It is a very steep climb up the grass hillside to the top of the ridge. Take a few breathers as you make your way up this 45° slope and take in the splendour of the beautiful Devon valley opening out behind you. As you get close to the top, the scene looking back widens out with a glimpse of the sea in Start Bay just showing between a dip in the hills.

At the top of the ridge a waymarker directs you through a gap in the high stone bank to the next field and a panoramic view of Lannacombe Bay. It is the views that make this climb worthwhile. Turn right and make your way up to the top right-hand corner of the field where a gate opens into a wide farm track. This farm track ends in a second

gate and the footpath keeps to the left-hand side of the next field continuing up the rise. Away to the right the vista over the brow of the rolling hills expands out to the heights of Dartmoor. After the next gate the footpath still keeps to the hedgerow and you can just see the top of the tower of South Allington church in the valley.

The bridleway is clearly signposted beyond the following gate and from here the water tower and houses of East Prawle can be seen on the skyline. Signposts for the bridleway will direct you over a number of farm tracks to a T-junction just past the converted barn

**On the way to Lannacombe** ▲

Walking the coastal path from East Prawle to Lannacombe you pass Maelcombe House, an Edwardian mansion that stands in its own grounds. The shoreline of Lannacombe Bay comprises large expanses of flat bedrock interspersed with small shingle beaches backed by low cliffs. At Malcombe Point a short line of trees fringes the cliff.

complex at Higher Borough. **(G)** Turn left, still following the signs for the bridleway, and walk down this wide farm track to a cross-roads. Straight ahead is the private lane down to Lower Borough ending in the driveway to the house at Woodcombe Sand; the bridleway goes off to the right and as it crests a small ridge, there is a section of grooved concrete through a dip designed to give purchase to farm vehicles in slippery conditions.

Just before the farmstead at Woodcombe there is a notice announcing that the bridleway has been legally diverted around the farm and a signpost directs you across a field to the left. **(H)** Unfortunately, there is a large pond at the bottom of this field and the water running off from the farm at the top of the hill has created an impassable muddy quagmire that at times is more than knee deep. When conditions are bad hikers have no alternative but to take the original route through the farmyard. The track that circles the farm meets up again with the bridleway on the other side.

At the point where the legal diversion meets with the bridleway there is a signpost for the footpath to Woodcombe Sand ¾ mile, which is the other end of the short cut mentioned earlier. You can also see from this signpost that the distance walked from Lannacombe Green has been 1½ miles and that another ½ mile will complete the hike back to East Prawle.

Where the track splits **(I)** take the paved road into East Prawle. Turn left at the triangle of grass at the meeting of the roads, crossing to the footpath alongside Cooling's Farm. Beyond the farm the footpath steps to the right passing behind hedgerows at the back of a number of cottage gardens and comes out to a roadway in the middle of the village. Cross this road and go up the hill past the Providence Inn.

At the top turn left and walk back to the village green.

# 4 EAST PRAWLE TO MILL BAY

**Sunset at Prawle Point** ▲

Shadows spread across Prawle Point, the most southerly tip of Devon, as the sun sets beyond Bolt Head, lighting vapour trails in the sky. This aerial view emphasises the remoteness of the cottages once home to the Coastguards that manned the Coast Watch Station on the exposed headland.

**Langerstone Point** ▲

Fish-in-the-well Rock and Lobeater Rock form the escarpment beyond the old Coastguard cottages. On the seashore, wide platforms of rock are scalloped into tiny coves and the long finger of Langerstone Point reaches out to sea. Start Point can be seen in the distance on the far side of Lannacombe Bay.

**The 'Demetrios'**

On the 18th December 1992 a vicious storm parted the towlines of the Greek cargo ship 'Demetrios' that was being towed on her last voyage to a breaker's yard in the Mediterranean. Gale force winds drove her on to the rocks to the west of Prawle Point where she broke her back and sat straddled across the reef. Thousands of sightseers flocked to witness the spectacle of such a large ship left stranded on the shore.

There was no threat of pollution from the empty ship and she was cut up for scrap. A tangle of plates lies on the seabed, and at low water spring tides the engine block with its rows of pistons is still exposed.

## THE COASTLINE

Prawle Point, with the old Coastguard station sitting on top, is the most southerly tip of Devon. From the wide rock platforms of Langerstone Point lying to the east, the small archway at the base of Prawle Point is clearly visible. The low fragile cliffs of sand, gravel and pebbles that run the full length of Lannacombe Bay now give way to the dramatic headlands of Prawle Point, Gammon Head and the Pig's Nose, with high, storm-resistant walls of Devonian green schist rising sheer from the sea. The shore from Start Point to Prawle Point and beyond to Gammon Head and Gara Rock is designated a Site of Special Scientific Interest. It is not only important for geological studies, but the unique habitats of the littoral zone with its bedrock platforms, the grasslands, the escarpments and exposed tors, are home to rare lichens, plants, insects and birds. Prawle Point is also first landfall for many migratory birds.

This is a very hazardous place for shipping and wrecks from as long ago as the Bronze Age have been found at Moor Sands below the Pig's Nose. The most recent wreck to founder on this section of the coast was the cargo vessel 'Demetrios' that broke up on Prawle Point during a storm in 1992.

Some of the most beautiful sandy coves and beaches are to be found between Prawle Point and The Bar at the entrance to Salcombe Harbour and the fine sands extend further along the eastern shores of the estuary as far up as Ditch End beyond the ferry slipway.

Good arable farmland covers the downs of the high plateau, and west of Gara Rock the more gentle sea-facing slopes are covered in coarse grass and shrubs. In the shelter of the estuary trees grow right down to the water's edge.

**Bronze Age Wreck**

The seabed off Moor Sands is of significant importance both historically and archaeologically. Bronze Age artefacts were found close inshore in 1977 comprising the blades of swords, axe heads, tools and ornaments that may have come from one of the oldest wrecks ever discovered, dating from 1300 BC.

In 1995 a group of divers unearthed a large collection of Islamic treasure close to the same site. An expanded search of the seabed uncovered more Bronze Age relics in 2005.

The area of these discoveries has been placed under the Protection of Wrecks Act 1973 to guard against unauthorised, illegal and opportunist diving.

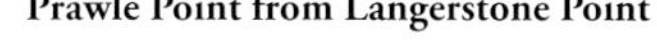

**Prawle Point from Langerstone Point**

**Elender Cove** ▲

Elender Cove is tucked away under the high crags of Gammon Head. This is an idyllic sandy cove accessible by a steep climb down from the coastal path. The cove is a favourite overnight anchorage for yachts during quiet weather with offshore winds.

## ACCESSIBLE BEACHES AND COVES

### 1. Horsley Cove

(Access Level 3)

This is a gravel and shingle beach tucked into a corner of the cliffs below where the footpath from East Prawle meets the coastal path under Sharper's Head. It is accessed by a track that descends through a cleft in the low crumbling cliffs. At the bottom of the path turn right and walk along the beach to the corner where the cliffs start to rise higher.

There is a rocky foreshore in front of the beach but a shingle channel between the rocks opens out for swimming. The cove is sheltered from the currents around Prawle Point but care should be taken not to swim too far from shore. The gravel beach remains exposed at high tide.

### 2. Elender Cove

(Access Level 4)

A beautiful sandy beach at the base of Gammon Head with a cave in the cliff face is the reward for the effort of the challenging climb down from the coastal path that is very steep in places. Although there is no beach remaining at high tide, as the tide recedes a wide expanse of fine sand opens up and the cove is great for swimming. It is a very popular anchorage for private yachts. The nearest parking is at The National Trust car park at Prawle Point. From the car park, walk back up the hill and then take the farm track off to the left at the sharp bend in the road.

### 3. Moor Sands

(Access level 4)

Moor Sands lies at the bottom of a wide curving expanse of sloping hillside bounded to the east by the headland of the Pig's Nose. It is a coarse sand and gravel beach with large rocks and boulders. Swimming is safe close to the beach but there are large rocks in the water and strong currents run offshore.

Access to the beach is by a steep track down the side of the Pig's Nose headland. The coastal path traverses midway up the hillside behind Moor Sands and Venerick Cove.

The beach is quite remote and best reached from the car park at Gara Rock.

### 4. Rickham Sands

(Access Level 3)

Rickham Sands is now less popular since the Gara Rock Hotel has disappeared, with the loss of its facilities. It is a good sandy beach with safe bathing. The steady walk down from the car park in the field at Gara Rock and the struggle back after a day on the beach, will be tiring for young children.

There is ample beach remaining at high water, but unfortunately, the sand is littered with plastic bottles and containers washed up by the tide.

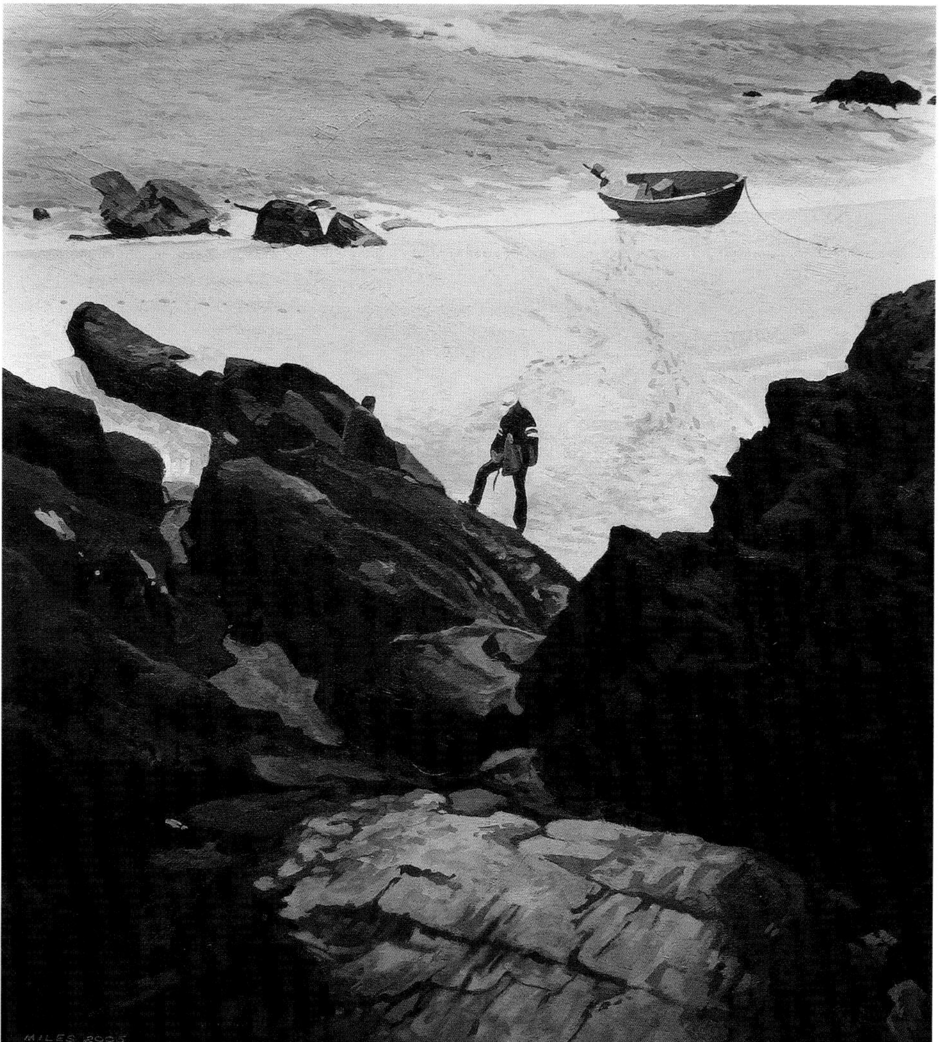


**Gara Rock Hotel**

Alas no more! The loss of no other hotel in the South Hams has been mourned as much as the demolition and removal of the Gara Rock Hotel above Rickham Sands. Originally this was the site of Rickham Coastguard Station that was converted to a hotel that had its halcyon days in the 1930's. If the truth be known it was not the loss of the hotel that spurred the campaign to keep it open, but the demise of the bar and tea garden so popular with hikers on the coastal path and holiday makers visiting the beach. Fond memories linger on of sunny afternoons eating cream teas on the terrace. Whichever way you look at it, a modern apartments complex is never going to hold the same appeal for the public.

**Deep Discussion below Gara Rock** ▲

The golden beach of Rickham Sands is a short walk down from Gara Rock at the east end of Portlemouth Down.

**General notes for the beaches of East Portlemouth**

The beaches on the east side of the estuary can best be reached by the Salcombe – East Portlemouth passenger ferry that operates a daily service all year round from Salcombe town quay (ferry steps) to the East Portlemouth slipway. (8.00am – 5.30pm)

Alternatively there is a National Trust car park for approximately 80 cars in the tree lined valley behind Mill Bay. However, it is a torturous route to reach this car park along narrow country lanes with passing places, that takes you from Frogmore on the A379 via South Pool to East Portlemouth.

A café and public toilets are located above the ferry slipway.

At low spring tides it is possible to walk along an unbroken stretch of sand from the ferry slipway to Mill Bay. At extreme low tides you can continue along the beach around Biddlehead Point to Sunny Cove. At high water the only beaches left exposed and accessible are at Mill Bay and Sunny Cove. Small's Cove retains an area of dry sand at high tide but it is backed by private properties and becomes effectively cut off.

**5. Sunny Cove**

(Access Level 2)

To reach this small cove walk along the coastal path from Mill Bay. It stands at the mouth of the estuary facing south-west looking out across The Bar to Bolt Head.

It has a beautiful fine sandy beach that shelves gently into the water flanked by rocks. The tidal flow can cause strong rip currents and swimmers should not venture too far from the beach.

**6. Mill Bay**

(Access Level 1)

A paved road connects the ferry slipway to Mill Bay. At the back of the beach is a National Trust car park, where there are also public toilets.

This beach is a paradise for children, with fine golden sand, rock pools and a stream that flows down the beach under the spreading branches of mature trees. On the opposite side the sand is banked up to a rock ledge where upturned dinghies are stored. A large expanse of beach remains at high tide.

Swimming is safe but care should be taken at low water when the tidal pull of the estuary will be felt.

The view across the estuary is of large houses and mansions ranged across the steep wooded hillside and the constant stream of water traffic adds colour and interest to the scene.

Dogs are allowed on the beach but since it is fairly compact they should be kept under control.

**Salcombe - East Portlemouth Ferry**

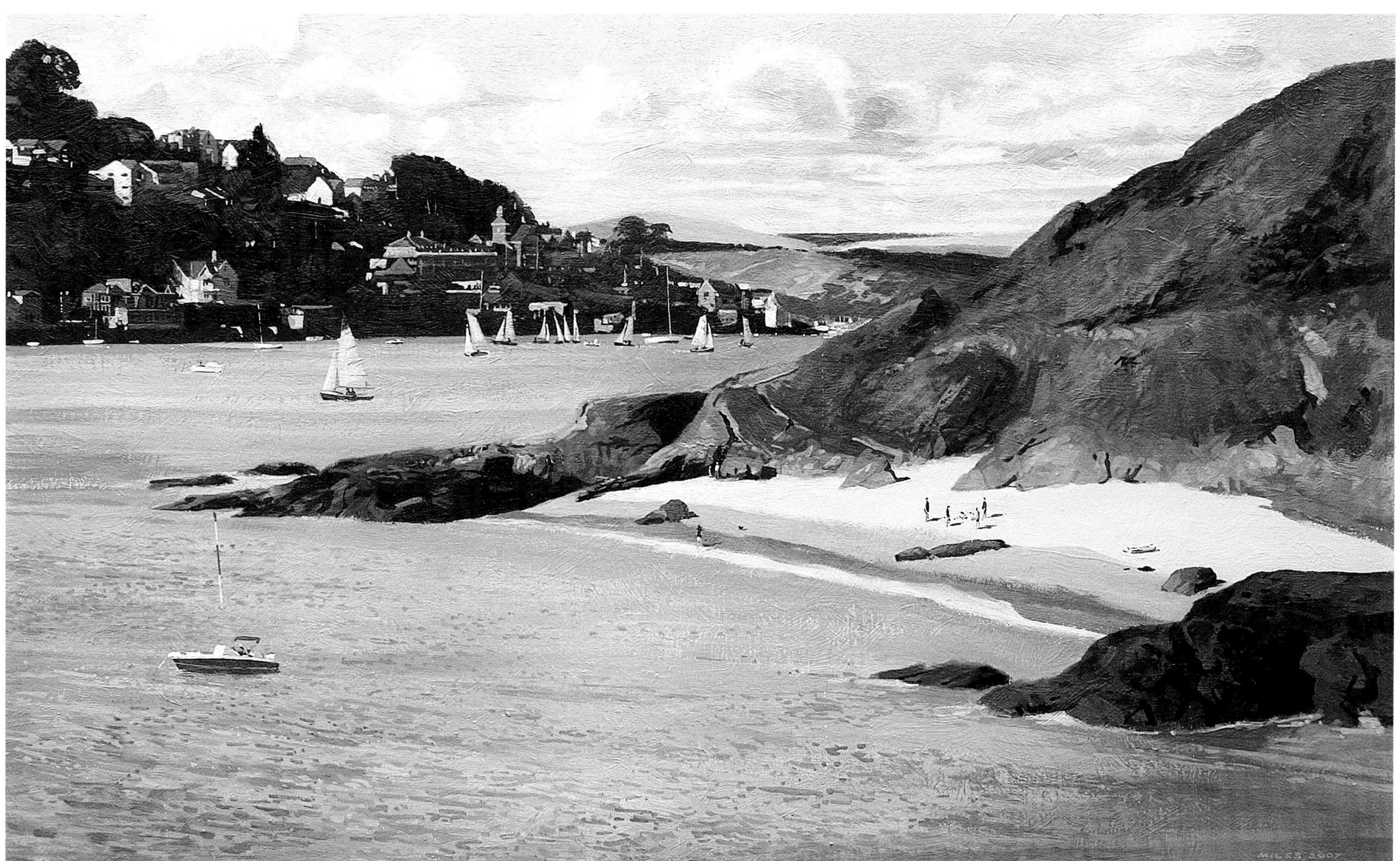

**Sunny Cove** ▲

This sandy beach on the East Portlemouth side of Salcombe Harbour can be reached by walking the coastal path from Mill Bay. A passenger ferry connects this quiet, undeveloped shoreline with the bustling waterfront of Salcombe.

## WALK 7 PRAWLE POINT

| | |
|---|---|
| **Distance** | **4 miles** |
| **Time** | **2¼ hours** |
| **Grade** | **3** |

The walk starts at East Prawle village green. **(A)**

The first stage of this walk is shared with Walk 6.

Leave the village green along the no-through road to the right of Grunter's Café that wends its way down towards the coast. Prawle Point comes into view as the road gets steeper and bends to the right. The footpath passes down the side of Bayfield, the last cottage of the row of houses on the left.

The path slopes gently downhill between high hedgerows. (Part way down the path, before you reach the T-junction, there is a stone stile set into the wall on the left. This is a short cut that crosses the corner of the field. The short cut is steep and gets slippery in wet conditions.) If you continue to the bottom of the hill you turn left and are treated to a view of Lannacombe Bay with the wide ledges of Gorah Rocks in the foreground.

This wider stony track with a water gully down the left hand side has high banks and hedges that frame the picture of the bay ahead. After bearing to the left the path gets steeper and more uneven.

Pass through a five bar gate into a field where the path splits on either side of a hedgerow that separates two fields. Although the signpost indicates that the path is right of the hedge, the beaten track is on the left. At the far end of the field there is a signpost to Prawle Point 1¼ miles. **(B)**

There is a narrow path that descends to the beach, used to launch the upturned boats lying in the field. This path is also access to Horseley Cove, tucked away in the corner under Sharpers Head. The coastal path follows the edge of the field inside the line of bracken, bramble and scrub that grows along the top of the low cliffs. The well-marked path rounds the base of the headland and eventually a gate opens into a grass field. A notice asks for dogs to be kept on the lead to avoid disturbing grazing sheep.

The whole shoreline is platform rocks interspersed with coarse sand and gravel, strewn with driftwood and flotsam thrown up high upon the shore by storms. Once around Sharpers Head, Prawle Point, the southernmost tip of Devon, stands before you with the distinctive Coast Watch Station on top and a natural stone arch at its base.

There are now two stiles to be scaled, the first a wooden stile and the second a stonework stile. Beyond the second stile the shoreline becomes more accessible and there are places where you can scramble down to the platforms of Brimpool Rocks and

**Prawle Point**

Langerstone Point, an extending finger that reaches out towards Prawle Point. A wider stretch of gravel forms a small beach.

Through the next gate you enter a field where the path splits. Go straight ahead crossing the field to a five bar gate. (The path going diagonally across the field to the right goes up to a stile at the head of a lane that runs down from East Prawle. In this lane you find The National Trust car park that can be used as an alternative starting Point for the walk.) **(C)**

The coastal path climbs the next field to a gate in a stone wall at the top of the ridge, passing a row of cottages up on the right that were once the homes of the Coastguards that manned the station on Prawle Point. Sheep graze regularly on these grassy slopes and again dog owners should take special care not to startle them.

Cross the rough grass to the Coast Watch Station and Visitors Centre **(D)** now manned by the volunteers from the National Coastwatch Institution. The views from Prawle Point in both directions are stunning; to the left Lannacombe Bay looking out to Start Point and to the right Bolt Head and the entrance to Salcombe Harbour.

Moving on from the Coast Watch Station the coastal path first wends its way over grassy slopes but soon becomes more rugged as it traverses high rock cliffs and there is a stone stile and a bit of a scramble down the side of Signalhouse Point.

The path now becomes steeper and somewhat more difficult as it zigzags its way down the face of the cliff in order to negotiate a large outcrop where you climb through a gap in the rock. Steps have been cut in several places to make the passage a little easier. After rounding the corner of Signalhouse Point you see Elender Cove at the foot of Gammon Head, one of the finest views along this stretch of the coast.

Once past the rocks the path becomes gentler as it rises through heather and bracken towards the back of the bay and then levels out. The path rises again above Elender Cove, tucked into the corner of Gammon Head. **(E)** Here two footpaths meet and you turn right and walk back along the higher track until you reach the first footpath leading off

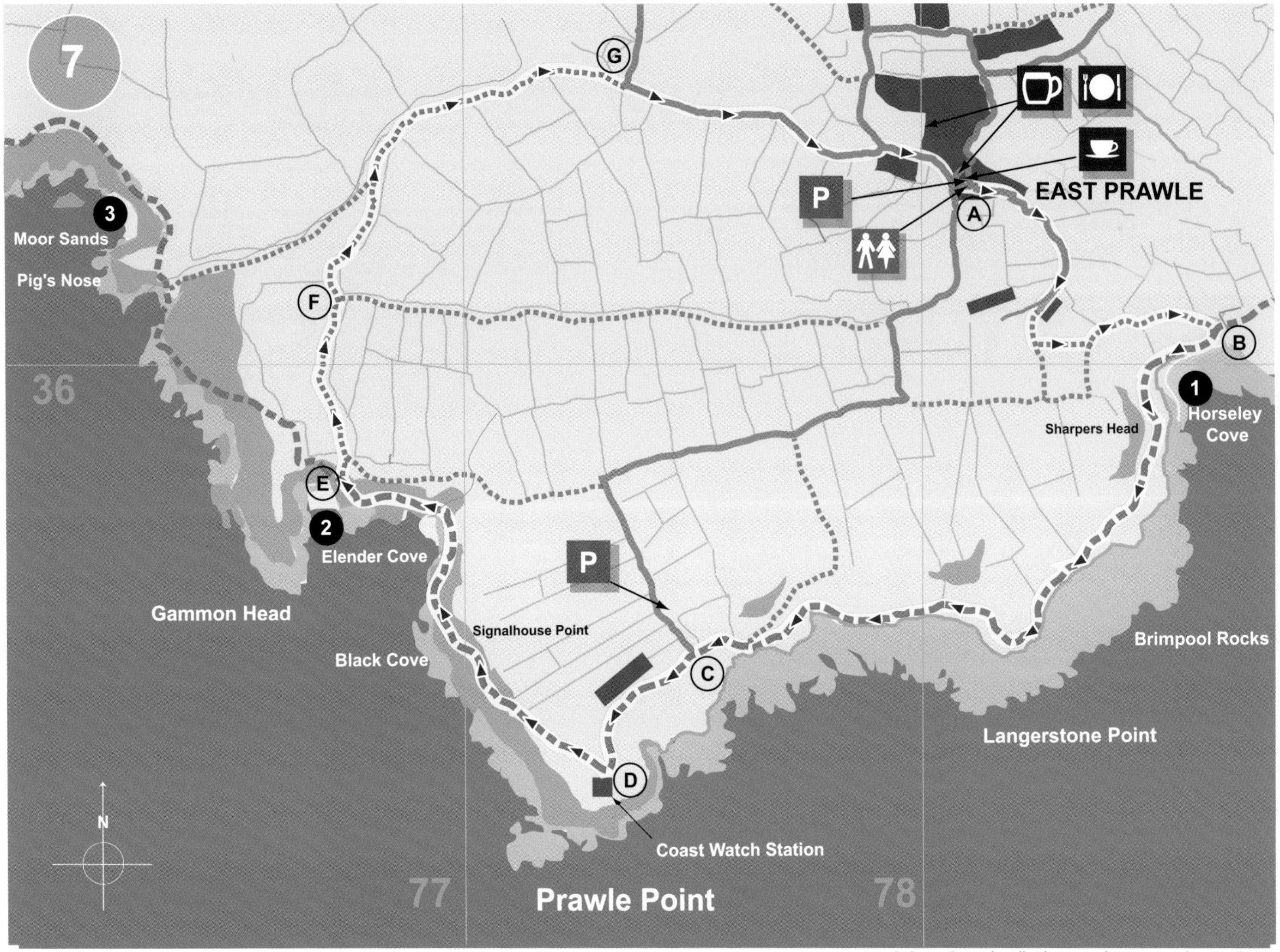

7
G
EAST PRAWLE
A
P
Moor Sands
Pig's Nose
F
B
36
Sharpers Head
Horseley Cove
E
Elender Cove
P
Gammon Head
Signalhouse Point
Black Cove
C
Brimpool Rocks
Langerstone Point
D
N
Coast Watch Station
77
Prawle Point
78



to the left. This is a steady climb up a sunken path with a stone wall on the left that runs inland away from the cliffs. Halfway up the rise there is a stile and at the top a bridleway to the right offers a short cut back to East Prawle. **(F)**

Go straight on, eventually reaching a farm gate beyond which there is a wide grass path edged with stone. Looking back down the valley, attractive views open up across the mouth of the Salcombe-Kingsbridge Estuary to Bolt Head and Sharp Tor. After the next five bar gate a stony track winds its way uphill to a paved road where you turn right towards East Prawle. **(G)**

Upon entering the village turn right at the T-junction and the road takes you back to the village green.

**Coast Watch Station.**

The Maritime and Coastguard Agency (MCA) maintained and manned a lookout on Prawle Point until 1992, the station being finally closed in 1994 having been replaced by modern technology. The line of Coastguard cottages to the east of the station that are now holiday homes and lets, shows that there was a large workforce of highly trained personnel needed to keep the lookout fully manned for 24 hours, 365 days of the year.

Following the deaths of two fishermen off Lizard Point in 1994 in full view of a derelict coastguard lookout platform the National Coastwatch Institute (NCI), a voluntary charity organisation, was formed to reinstate visual maritime surveillance around the coast of Britain. The NCI renovated, equipped and reopened Prawle Point Coast Watch Station in April 1998 and now some 60 volunteers, trained to MCA standards, scan the seaways with powerful telescopes and radar, monitor radio channels, and keep a check on sea and weather conditions, providing a valuable contribution to the safety of yachts, fishing vessels and diving boats that might get into difficulties.

The lookout has an information centre telling everything about its history and present day functions.

## WALK 8 GARA ROCK

**Distance** 3 miles
**Time** 1¾ hours
**Grade** 1

The walk starts at The National Trust car park at Mill Bay. **(A)**

The car park lies between the trees in the valley behind Mill Bay where there are public toilets.

Walk through the car park to the five bar gate at the top and on along the track that leads up the side of the valley under a canopy of mature trees. You can hear a small stream trickling over the stones to your left as it tumbles down to the beach. Even on the warmest days in summer the thick lush foliage overhead provides constant shade as you make your way up this wide and even path.

The next gate opens into a farm track **(B)** and the farm and cottages at Rickham can be seen through the trees across the valley to the left. Cross the track and take the steps up to a second five bar gate bearing the notice, "This land is being managed by the Countryside Stewardship Scheme". A narrow sunken footpath continues uphill between stone walls clad with ivy and tall hedgerows. Ferns and other plants that favour this damp and shady habitat grow lushly by the side of

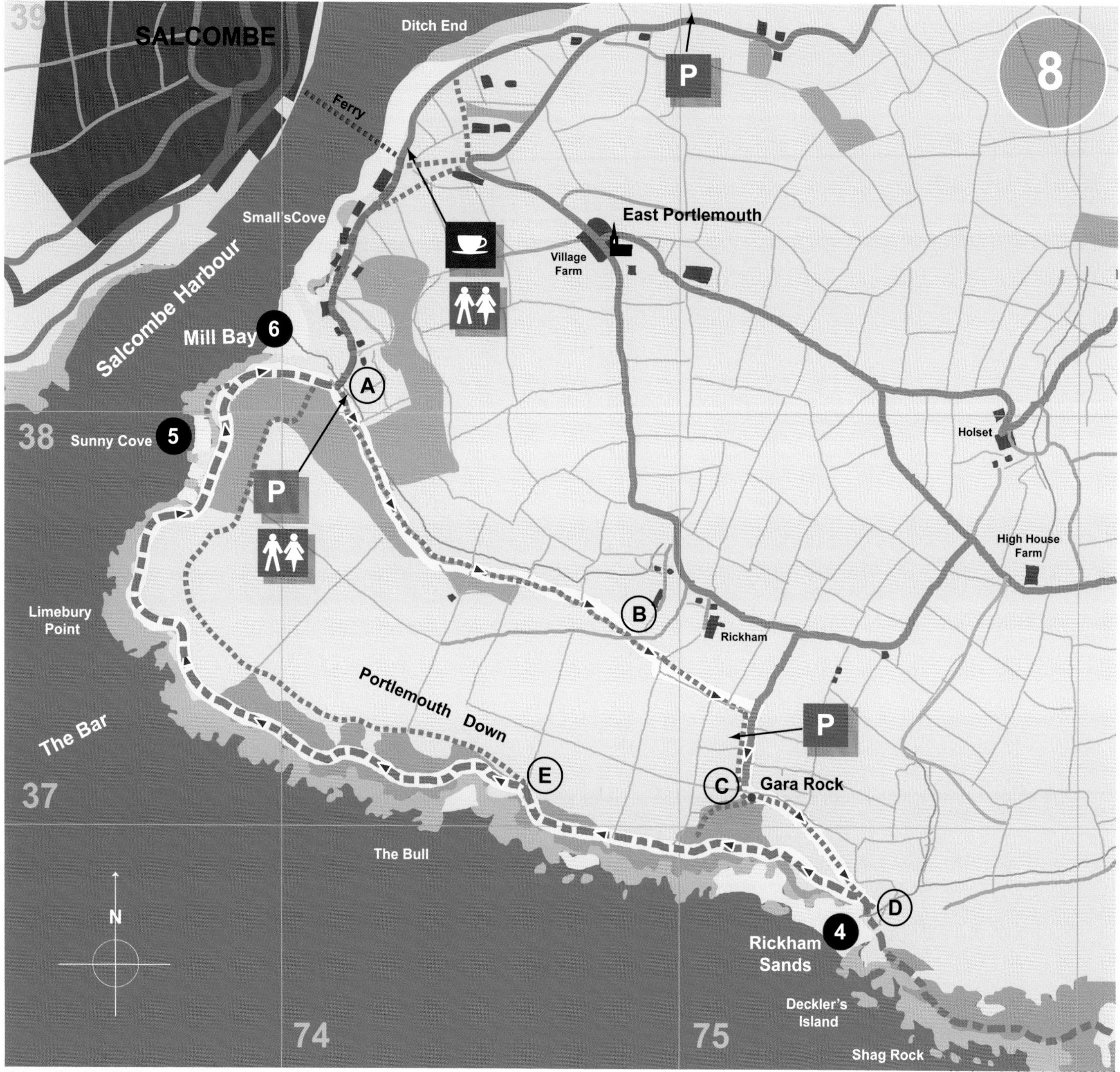



the path. In early spring the left-hand bank is blanketed with primroses.

Beyond the next gate the walk enters the open fields of Portlemouth Down and the track goes diagonally over a field between the crops. At the far side of the second field the footpath meets the country lane out to Gara Rock where the hotel once stood. **(C)**

There is a pay car park inside the field and you can walk down the cinder track to the coastal path and the tiny huer's hut hanging over the cliff edge. Towers such as this were used to spot shoals of pilchard. The lookout would raise the cry that fish had been sighted and when the fishing boats were launched he would signal to direct them towards the catch. There was once a Coastguard station here and this vantage point was used in later years as a watchtower.

(At the time of writing the Gara Rock Hotel has been demolished and the site is to be redeveloped.)

A signpost at the huer's hut gives the walk back to Mill Bay at 2¼ miles, but if it is a nice day, carry on down the cliff path to Rickham Sands, **(D)** before returning along the lower coastal path. Looking straight ahead as you walk down to the beach the first headland is the Pig's Nose and the second Gammon Head.

The walk above the cliff tops from Rickham Sands back to Mill Bay provides a continuous glorious view and an ever-widening panorama that includes Bolt Head, the heights of Sharp Tor and the mouth of Salcombe Harbour. On hazy days the jagged rocks of The Rags can be seen silhouetted against the dark backdrop of Stairhole Bay. The coastal path

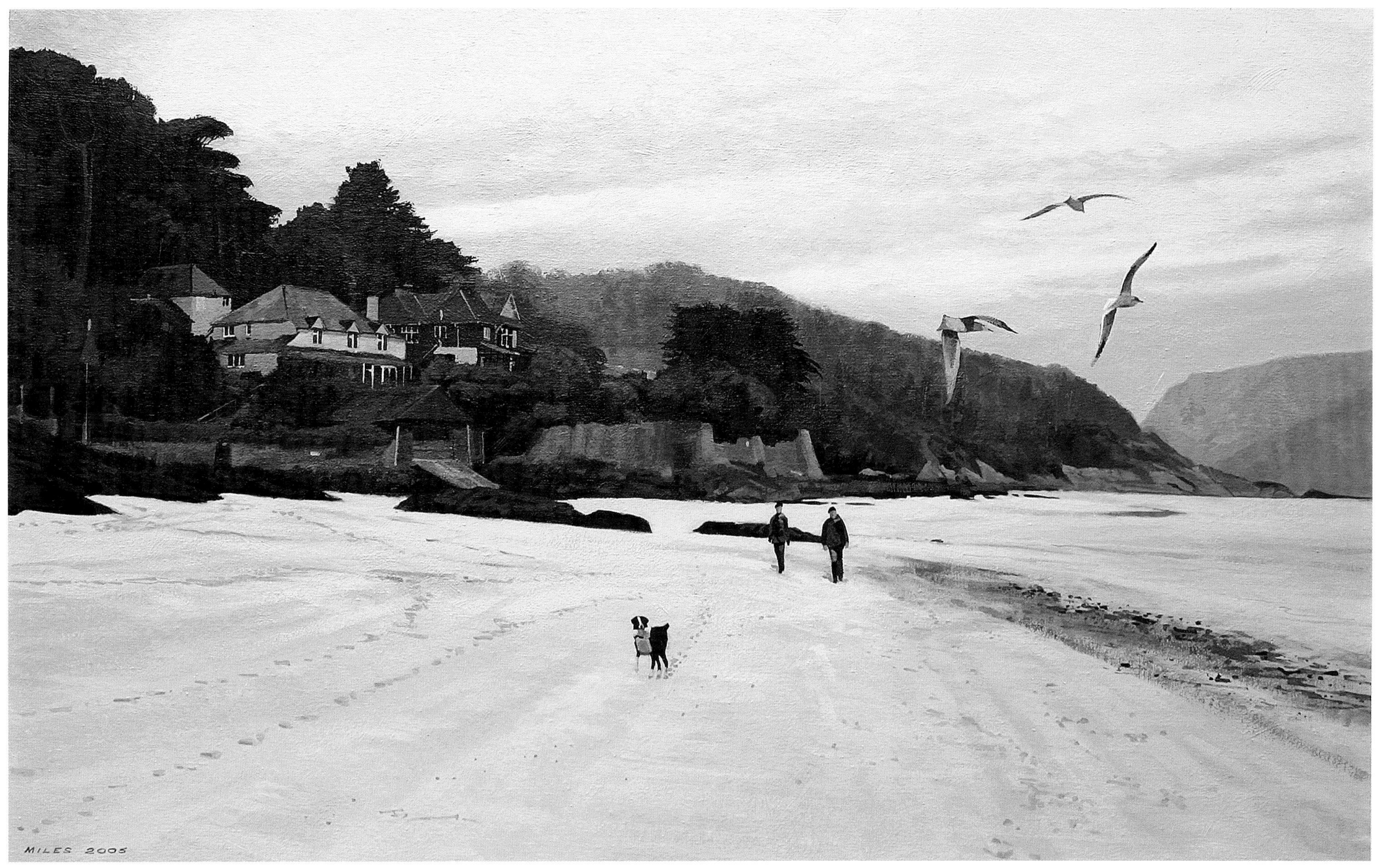


**Winter's Ebb – Small's Cove** ▲

During low water spring tides, Salcombe Harbour exposes wide expanses of sand banks and the waters of the estuary narrow to a shallow channel. At these times it is possible to walk uninterrupted along the sandy beach on the East Portlemouth side from the ferry jetty right out beyond Biddlehead Point to Sunny Cove, passing Small's Cove and Mill Bay along the way.

below Gara Rock is very well maintained by The National Trust and has been widened in several places.

The path splits **(E)** and you can take either the upper path along the edge of Portlemouth Down or the lower coastal path that takes a mid-level route along the cliff face. Several short cuts down the hillside link the two paths along the way. The lower coast path starts fairly smooth and level but later there are one or two scrambles as it skirts around the back of tiny coves. The path then levels out again and turns gradually into the entrance to Salcombe Harbour. The first turn in the path brings South Sands into view on the other side of the estuary. The path then gradually loses height and drops closer to the rocky foreshore. North Sands with the ruins of Fort Charles appears as you top a small rise above Sunny Cove and promptly disappears as you enter a copse. You catch glimpses of Salcombe through the branches as the path works its way down through the trees to Mill Bay.

**The Huer's Hut - Gara Rock**

5

## SALCOMBE - KINGSBRIDGE ESTUARY

▲ **Salcombe**

The tower of Holy Trinity Church is framed by Southpool Creek and dominates the skyline when viewing the town from the advantage of Bonfire Hill.

Salcombe Yawls

Salcombe was historically a remote, seafaring port at the mouth of a tidal estuary, reliant on the sea for its commerce and communication. This small township saw traditional shipbuilding flourish for a time in the mid 19th century in support of a successful trade in the import of fruit from the Bahamas, the Mediterranean and the Azores and the export of local produce such as corn, flour, wool and potatoes.

The Industrial Revolution gave birth to steam engines and steel hulled ships, and the large commercial shipyards that sprang up close to the coalfields and iron foundries brought about the demise of Salcombe's wooden shipbuilding and its associated trades. Boat building and boat repair workshops remain in Salcombe on a very small scale along Island Street. The new development of Hannaford's Landing on Island Quay has workshops on the ground floor but does not signify a revival in small boat building. The only reflection of Salcombe's past maritime glory is in the architecture of 18th and 19th century houses and mansions built by prosperous merchants, ship builders and sea captains.

It was not until the Great Western Railway came to Kingsbridge in 1893 that Salcombe's unique and beautiful, southernmost location, mild climate and wonderful leisure sailing opportunities, awakened the town's tourist potential. Today, Salcombe is a bit of a paradox with stark contrasts between its summer and winter guise.

In summer the town is a thriving sailing and boating Mecca, with the harbour and its moorings filled to capacity. The waters of the estuary sparkle in the wake of the many yachts, dinghies and powerboats that sail constantly to and fro. Clothing shops sport nautical names and the styles of the clothes pander to the sailing fraternity, while chandlers supply the cleats, ropes, pulleys and paraphernalia to keep their boats shipshape.

Summer visitors include those who come just to savour the atmosphere and quaintness of this attractive old harbour town, and sunworshippers that take full advantage of the beautiful sandy beaches on either side of the estuary, using the Salcombe to East Portlemouth passenger ferry to get across to the other side. For the sailing enthousiasts, boats of all shapes and sizes can be hired to explore the backwaters of the estuary, and there are boat trips organised for fishing and diving. The old lifeboat 'Joseph Soar' runs trips out to sea beyond The Bar and the 'River Maid' sails daily between Salcombe and Kingsbridge throughout the summer months.

Good pubs, restaurants and cafés abound in the cramped town centre where unwelcome cars edge their way gingerly through narrow streets between overflowing pavements. Car parking is costly and at a premium although the recent addition of a bus park-and-ride service does something to ease the congestion and makes Salcombe more accessible.

The extraordinary beauty of its location coupled with a mild climate has also made Salcombe a mecca for retirement and the town has an ageing population and a very high percentage of second homes and holiday accommodation. When the boisterous echoes of summer stop reverberating on its walls the town falls under an unnatural hush. In winter Salcombe can be explored at leisure but the place does have a somewhat dormant air, as if it is waiting for the metamorphosis into its summer colour and vitality.

**The Salcombe Yawl**

This is a classic clinker-built boat made from mahogany planking with wooden masts and spars and varnished decks. The two-mast rig with a mizzen sail has its roots in small fishing vessels that were used for crabbing and inshore fishing in the latter part of the 19th century. They were first built in the 1930s and craftsmen at small boatyards in Salcombe, Beer and Exmouth continue to build them using traditional wooden boat building techniques.

The Salcombe Yawl has long been a favourite for dinghy racing and is a recognised sailing class, governed by the Salcombe Yawl Owners Association. There have been design improvements over the years and now the older vessels are raced separately from the newer ones, being split into a Blue Fleet and Red Fleet respectively.

It is a lovely sight to see them gathered in numbers in the estuary on race days and regattas.

**Salcombe from Snapes Point** ►

Salcombe harbour shimmers in the afternoon light and the terraces of houses rising up the steep hillside are in shadow. High tide floods the mouth of the estuary and summer haze shrouds the heights of Sharp Tor.

MILES 2004

Salcombe Waterfront

**Salcombe Maritime and Local History Museum**

It is not surprising that a museum in Salcombe should focus on the town's history as a sailing port. In the 19th century some of the world's finest and sleekest high-speed schooners were built in boatyards in Salcombe Harbour. The importing of fresh fruit from as far away as the Bahamas relied upon the shortest possible sailing schedules and these vessels with skeleton crews ran enormous risks to bring citrus fruit back to home markets. Needless to say there were high losses in ships and crews.

The museum's collections include paintings and photographs of locally built and owned ships, together with models of ships, and examples of ships logs, wooden boat building tools, and insights into the art of sail making and rope making.

The wreck and rescue section has artefacts from shipwrecks, including a survivor's account of the disastrous wreck of the Salcombe Lifeboat 'William and Emma' that was caught by a freak wave as the crew rowed back across The Bar after trying to reach a stricken schooner.

The museum, in the base of the old Council Offices in Market Street, is open from Easter to the end of October.

## THE ESTUARY

The glaciers of the Ice Age did not reach the South Devon coast but the water from the melting ice scoured out the rolling hills and caused the sea level to rise and flood the valleys between Salcombe and Kingsbridge. It is normal for an estuary to be fed by a major river but here there are only tiny streams that barely dilute the seawater creating a very unusual marine environment.

The estuary with its many creeks also provides a recreational wonderland for sailing and boating and thousands of boats are moored against quays, jetties, pontoons and buoys throughout its length and breadth.

The estuary is protected against storm-wave action by the submerged sand bar at its mouth but the tidal range can reach 18 feet, filling and draining the whole area twice a day during spring tides. The wide variety of habitats, from the rich mud flats of the upper reaches, the surrounding farmland and wooded shores, down to the sandy beaches and rocky outcrops towards the open sea, attract many different species of resident and migratory birds. In the deep-water channel of Salcombe Harbour there are fields of eelgrass where recent studies have revealed two different species of seahorse. Cuttlefish and feather-stars can also be found among the fronds.

The future challenge for an estuary plan is to maintain a balance between the importance of leisure and tourism to the local economy and the need to conserve the ecology of these beautiful waterways that have been designated a Site of Special Scientific Interest.

**Kingsbridge Creek** ►

The Salcombe-Kingsbridge Estuary stretches some 6 miles inland along flooded valleys to Kingsbridge Quay. Little evidence of the industrial past remains from the time that this busy waterway was filled with the sounds of shipbuilding, and paddle steamers and sailing barges lined the wharves.

MILES 2004

Kingsbridge Market

## KINGSBRIDGE

Kingsbridge stands at the northernmost tip of the estuary. Even at this extremity the tidal differences are so great that at high tide you can step directly from the quayside onto the decks of the boats moored alongside, whereas 6½ hours later the boats rest on the mud 10 feet below and there is but a trickle of water left flowing down a channel in the middle of the inlet.

Why is it called Kingsbridge when there is no evidence of a bridge or apparent need for one? Hills rise away from the head of Kingsbridge Creek on all sides and the ordnance survey map shows at least four small streams converging on the Quay. In its natural state this area must have been marshland making a bridge necessary, but it has been long since transformed by land reclamation. The most impressive bridge in the area crosses Bowcombe Creek on the A379 linking Kingsbridge to West Charleton and Frogmore but this was not built until 1845.

Kingsbridge is a market town and the first settlement was probably established around the 12th century. When the Abbot of Buckfast became Lord of the Manor at Churchstow and gained control of the surrounding estates, he was granted a charter in 1219 to hold a market here for the sale of the produce from Buckfast Abbey, and since then markets have been held at Kingsbridge down through the ages. Even today there is a farmer's market on the quay next to the tourist office on the first Saturday of each month and general markets are held every week.

Another tradition is the Annual Kingsbridge Fair held on the 20th July, St. Margaret's Day, in accordance with a decree and charter from Henry VI in the 15th century. Since the revival of the Annual Fair in 1969 it now extends over a full week of events that include a fairground, a street procession and a firework display. The Fair is opened by the ceremony of hanging up a glove decorated with garlands but the origins of this tradition are lost in antiquity.

A pleasant diversity of shops line both sides of Fore Street, a steep one-way thoroughfare that runs uphill through the middle of the town. Behind many of the shop facades are much older buildings from as far back as the 15th century. These houses stood on long, narrow plots and as a consequence some shops are separated by very small alleyways that are interesting to explore.

St Edmund's Church and the Town Hall at the top of Fore Street are the most imposing buildings in the town. The Town Hall, built in 1850, once housed a butter and poultry market, as well as the police station and the assizes but it now incorporates the local cinema, a café and meeting rooms. Markets selling local produce and bric-a-brac are held in the foyer at regular intervals. The peculiar and unique three-faced clock surmounting the building has been reproduced on top of the Tourist Information Office on the Quay.

The top of the town including The Shambles, a low building supported on 8 stone columns, is the oldest part of the town dating from medieval times.

In the mid 1800s Kingsbridge shared with Salcombe the wealth of sea-borne trade, having its own shipyards, ropewalks, tanneries, cider breweries and corn mills. Paddle Steamers and barges plied up and down the estuary ferrying barley, leather, wool, flour and cider to the port at Salcombe and returned with fruit and coal. A branch line of the Great Western Railway brought further prosperity to the town, but the line has long since been removed and little remains of this industrial past. Kingsbridge has settled back into its origins as a pleasant and quiet unremarkable country market town.

**Cookworthy Museum**

William Cookworthy was a notable son of Kingsbridge who became an apothecary and developed high quality English porcelain from Cornish china clay. A collection of porcelain is on display in the museum.

The museum concentrates on the social history of Kingsbridge and its development as a market town and its collections are enhanced by being arranged over 9 galleries in a 17th century building that was once the Kingsbridge Grammar School. A panelled schoolroom has been preserved complete with the headmaster's seat with its impressive canopy and the Victorian school kitchen and scullery are fully equipped to re-create the period when the school catered for more than sixty boarders. Special displays are set up each year, and outside in a walled garden a collection of farm machinery and implements reflect life on the farm in the South Hams between the wars.

The museum is open from April to October.

**The Town Hall, St Edmund's Church and The Shambles**

KINGSBRIDGE
Heath Point
Kingsbridge Estuary
Lower Batson
Snapes Manor
Tosnos Point
Batson Creek
SALCOMBE
SNAPES POINT
9

## WALK 9 SNAPES POINT

| | |
|---|---|
| **Distance** | **4¼ miles** |
| **Time** | **2¼ hours** |
| **Grade** | **1** |

The walk starts at Shadycombe car park in Salcombe. **(A)**.

(Note: There is a shorter walk starting from The National Trust car park **(F)** missing out Batson Creek. This car park has a notorious reputation for car theft so if you choose to begin from here do not leave anything of value in the car.)

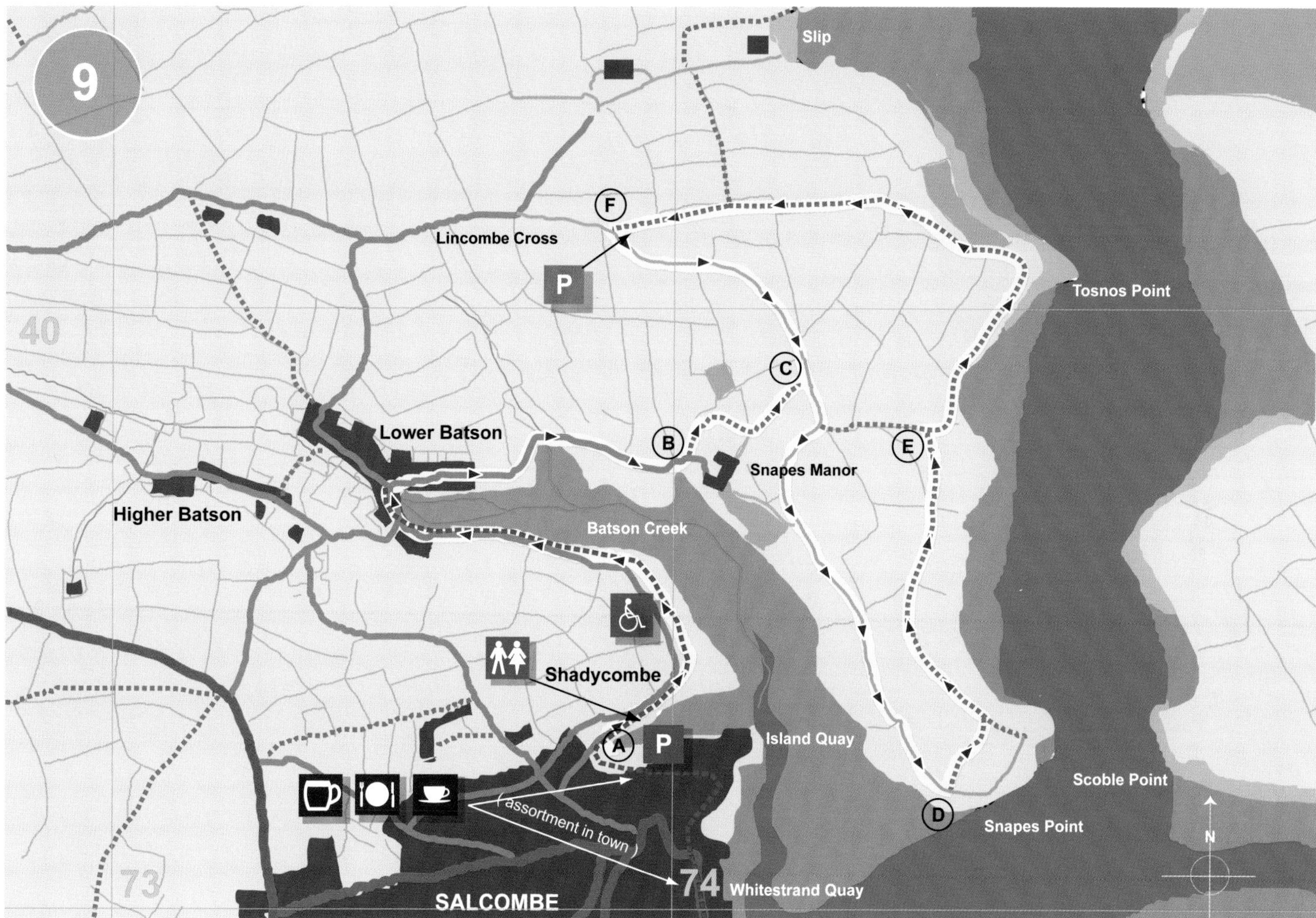




Walk from Shadycombe car park in the direction of Lower Batson. After the bend in the road you can strole along the grass verge that runs the length of Batson Creek. The large farmhouse on the opposite side is Snapes Manor. A little further along under overhanging trees are the remains of two limekilns on each side of the inlet.

Go around the head of the creek and if the tide is in, pause a while and sit on one of the seats on Lower Batson village green to soak up the atmosphere. The narrow lane down the other side of the creek first rises steeply between cottages and once over the brow descends back to the water's edge where there is a turning point beyond which there is no parking.

Walking further over the second hill brings you to the Manor House and just before you reach it take the footpath to the left. **(B)** A gate opens to a sunken track that goes up through trees and overlooks the garden. Passing through a second gate the footpath follows the lower edge of a field and enters a copse; here there are stepping-stones over a small brook that flows into the manor grounds. Exiting the woods the path crosses to the corner of a second field where it then turns left and climbs between ivy-clad banks until it meets a wide farm track at the top of the ridge. **(C)** A signpost gives Snapes Point to the right. Lying at her moorings in the stretch of estuary that has just come into view is the SS 'Egremond' an old Merseyside ferry that now serves as the headquarters of the Island Cruising Club, a sailing training organisation.

From here it is a very comfortable walk out to Snapes Point and as the hedgerow begins to thin, the track affords a superb panoramic view of Salcombe. This stretches from Bolt Head at the mouth of the estuary, right across the town and its waterfront as far as Batson Creek, and also encompasses East Portlemouth to Mill Bay on the other side of the harbour.

As you approach the main channel of the estuary, where the track bears left, there is a signpost to Snapes Point. **(D)** You go up a

MILES 2004

flight of stone steps to a gate with a notice telling you that you are entering National Trust property. Through the gate make your way up to the seat among the gorse bushes on the right. From here the view now includes Southpool Creek and Frogmore Creek and you can see the square tower of St Mary's Church in West Charleton on the skyline in the distance.

Skirt around the brow of the hill and follow the well-worn path to the gateway at the end of the field. The walk is now running parallel with the estuary in the direction of Tosnos Point. In the next field the footpath keeps to the lower line of old gnarled oaks above the water and you reach another gate. **(E)** There is a signpost for a path up the hill to the left but go straight on. As the walk continues along the water line the houses and the church at Kingsbridge come into view and to the right Wareham Point juts out into the channel at the mouth of Frogmore Creek. At low water the small rock reef of the Salt Stone is exposed.

The footpath now curves left following the boundary of the field and rises up the side of the hill. Halfway up you turn right through a gate in the hedge with a notice advising you that you are entering an area of "conservation walks" managed by the Countryside Stewardship Scheme. It explains that these are fields with open access linked by footpaths that are being managed without fertilizer to benefit wildlife. The path goes up the field to the left and it is a steady climb to the top of the ridge. According to the plan on the gate the footpath is supposed to keep to the left-hand side of this field but the worn track crosses diagonally to cut off a corner of projecting hedgerow. Across to the right the views of Kingsbridge and West Charleton broaden out.

A gate at the top opens to a gravel path to The National Trust car park. **(F)** In the car park is a plaque telling you about the walk and things to see and there is a viewpoint at the end with a picnic area equipped with tables and benches.

Leave the car park on the wide farm track in the direction of Snapes Point that returns you to the footpath back down the hill to Snapes Manor and Batson Creek.

**Moorings**

The creeks and channels of the estuary provide sheltered moorings for thousands of yachts and powerboats. This crowded pontoon is close to Tosnos Point. The upper creeks are only navigable 2 or 3 hours either side of high tide whereas boats moored in the main channel of Salcombe Harbour have the luxury of staying afloat at low water.

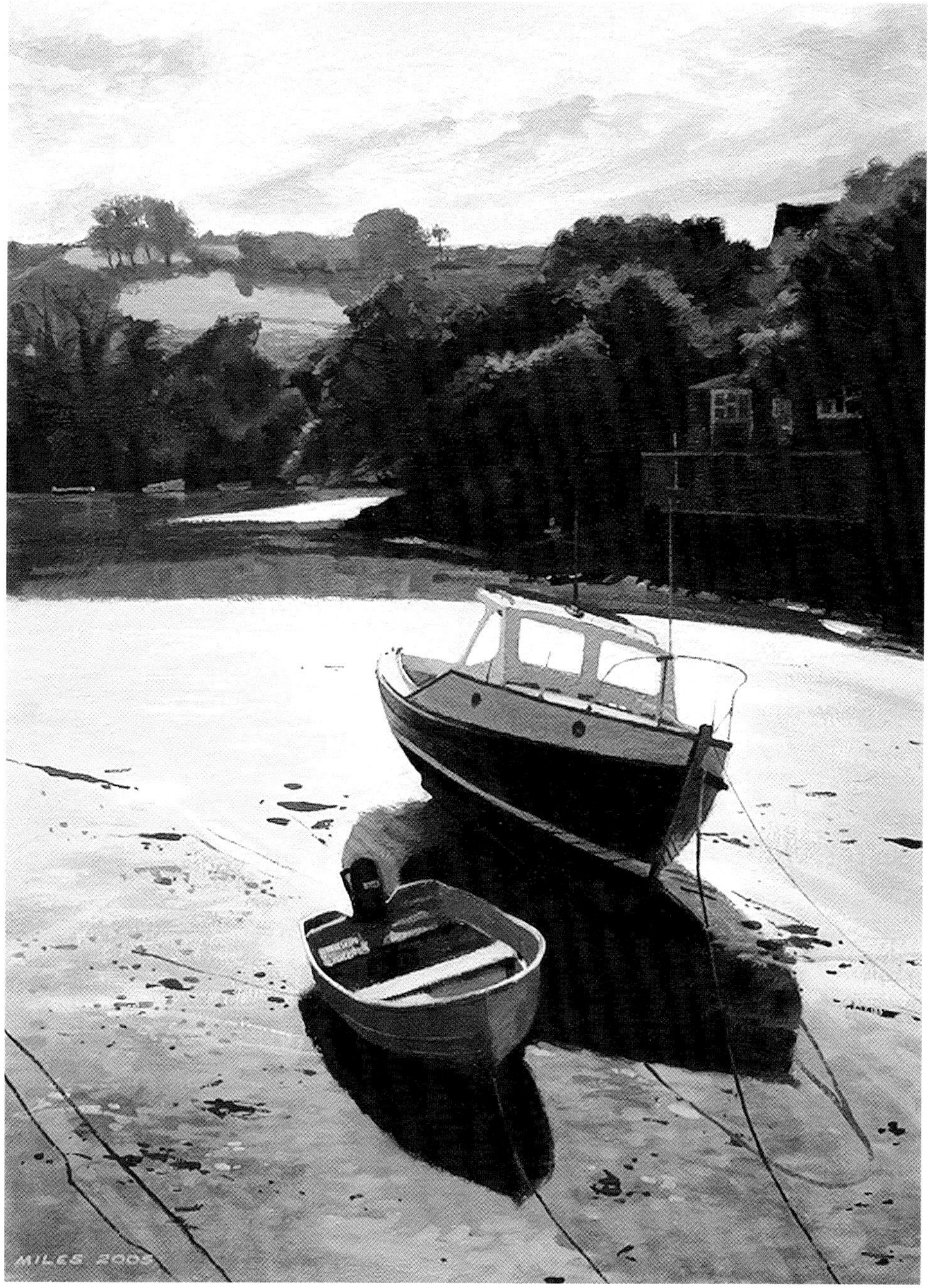

**Batson Creek** ►

The attractive hamlet of Lower Batson is only ten minutes walk from Salcombe. This was the site of a Saxon settlement long before Salcombe was established. At low tide the mud flats of Batson Creek glisten in the sunshine.

**Limekilns**

The Salcombe - Kingsbridge estuary is dotted with derelict limekilns once used for the burning and calcining of limestone for fertilizer. The kilns are all sited close to the water's edge since the coal and limestone had to be shipped in from Plymouth, there being no natural deposits of limestone or chalk in the South Hams.

The wide arch at the base of the kiln allowed a good draft of air for the conversion process and once the coal fire was started, limestone that had been broken down into small lumps by hand was fed into the kiln from the top. As the fire burned the lime was raked out of the bottom and riddled to separate the coal ash, then carted out to the farmsteads.

## WALK 10 FROGMORE CREEK

| | |
|---|---|
| **Distance** | **5¾ miles** |
| **Time** | **3½ hours** |
| **Grade** | **2** |

Note: Check the times of high water before starting this walk because the small section between **(D)** and **(E)** becomes flooded during high spring tides. Reckon on 45 minutes to get to this tidal section from Frogmore.

Park the car at the back of Frogmore Village Hall. **(A)**

Walk along the main road in the direction of Kingsbridge past the bakery and post office and up the hill to the Globe Inn. 100 yards beyond the pub on the left is a passageway between two houses signposted as a public footpath to Frogmore Creek 1¼ miles and West Charleton 2 miles. **(B)**

Pass through a gate, cross a small grass paddock and turn right along the creek over a stone stile. The footpath runs at the bottom of cottage gardens to a second stile into a field. Here you leave Frogmore village and although the footpath stays even and level above the creek side, a stile separates every field.

Eventually you come to an old stone barn where a three-way signpost points to Geese Quarries 1 mile. **(C)** This footpath goes down to the shore, passes around a standing stone and then crosses a small brook to a stone stile. Follow the track alongside the creek to a gate at the top of a rise. Further along the remnants of a limekiln stand on the opposite shore.

Stop and savour the tranquillity of this lovely creek. The banks and mudflats are alive with birds and the quiet is punctuated by song; the piping of oyster catchers, the mewing of gulls and in winter the haunting bubbling call of the curlew. At any time of year you will be able to see many different species of bird, even if you are not able to put a name to them.

Here again the path stays level but there are numerous stiles to be climbed before you reach the point that the path drops down onto the bed of Frogmore Creek. This is located at the end of a small field of long grass surrounded by a thicket of trees and scrub. The path turns left down a wooded ditch under overhanging branches. **(D)** A waymarker stands in the creek bed with an arrow pointing to the right. The path wends its way along the shore between rocks covered in bladder-wrack. It can be slippery in places so take care where you tread. At low water a sunken pontoon festooned in seaweed lies forlornly in the water.

After 200 yards of walking the creek bed, you come to a wide farm track going uphill to the right through the trees. **(E)** Here a signpost says simply public footpath and a notice warns that beyond this point the shores of the estuary are private for shooting and conservation, which would seem to be a contradiction!

The path climbs up through the woods around what used to be Geese Quarries but is now the landscaped gardens of a fashionable waterside property. At the top the path leaves the copse and crosses an open field to a

FROGMORE
WEST CHARLETON
East Charleton
Frogmore
Creek
Bowcombe Creek
Ham Point
Charleton Point
Wareham Point
KINGSBRIDGE ESTUARY
The Salt Stone
10

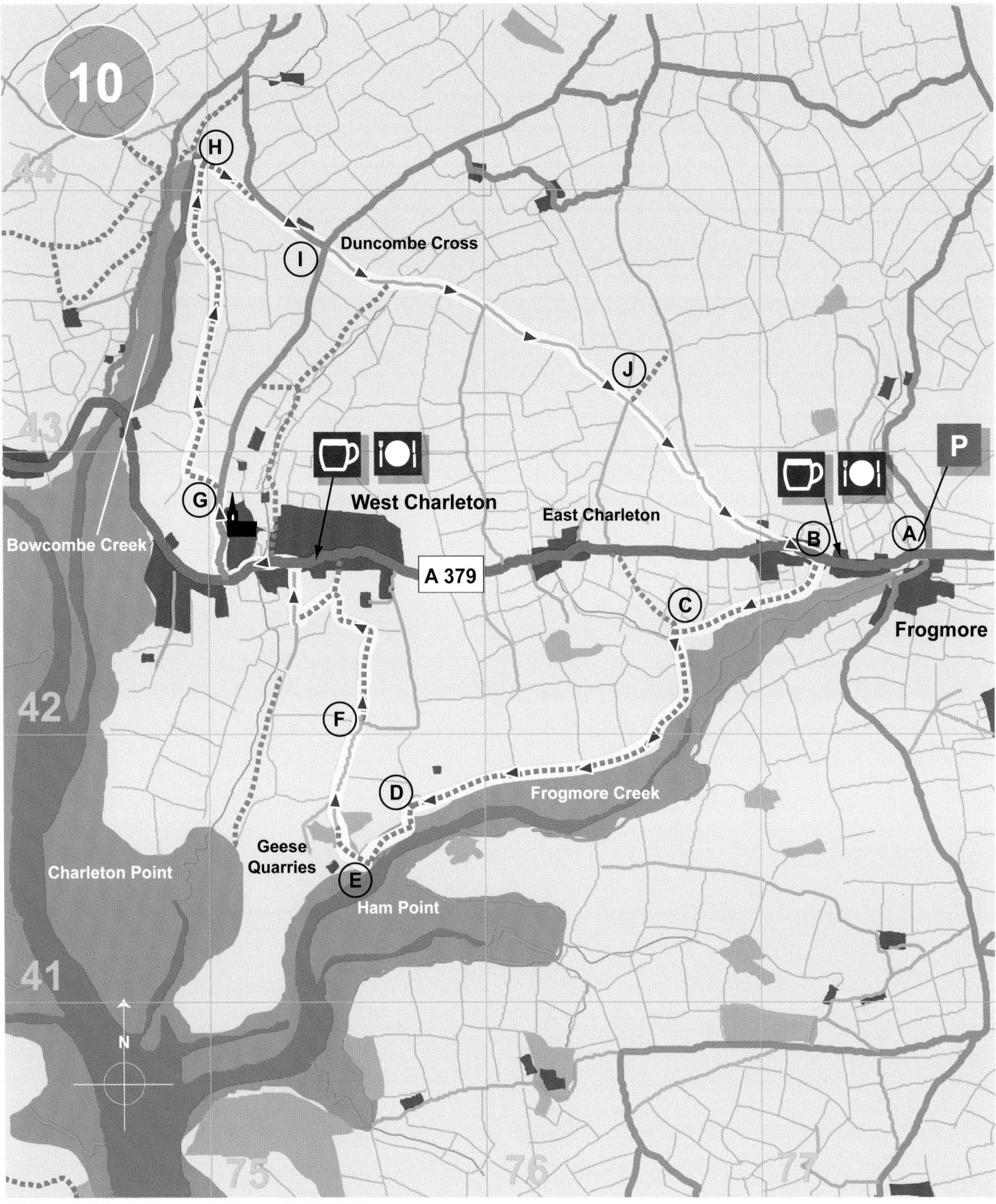




paved farm track. After 300 yards this lane turns sharply right where an iron beacon stands, erected by the villagers of Charleton in 1999 and lit on the 30th December to commemorate the 3rd millennium. **(F)**

Take the footpath through the farm gate that goes down the middle of the field between the crops towards the village of West Charleton below. At the bottom hedgerow the path turns left and then right over a stile into a paddock where ponies are often grazing. There are two exits from this field, one at the top with an alley passing between a row of houses and the other is through a farm gate into a lane at the left-hand side of the field; both connect to the main road.

At the A379 turn left, walk along the pavement up the hill, and cross over into Church Lane, which is a steady climb past St Mary's Church with its sturdy square Saxon tower. Take the first footpath to the left through a farm gate approximately 100 yards beyond the church. **(G)** There are garden allotments to the right as you enter the field and the path follows the fence to the bottom left-hand corner and around to a stile where the path comes to a stone wall. From here you can see the full sweep of the main channel of the estuary from Salcombe to Kingsbridge and below is the entrance to Bowcombe Creek. On the other side of the stile are the foundations of a demolished barn and the path continues at high level along the fence line to the right. As the footpath progresses along the ridge, looking back into the valley, Bowcombe Bridge comes into sight and you are privileged to see one of the most impressive views of the estuary.

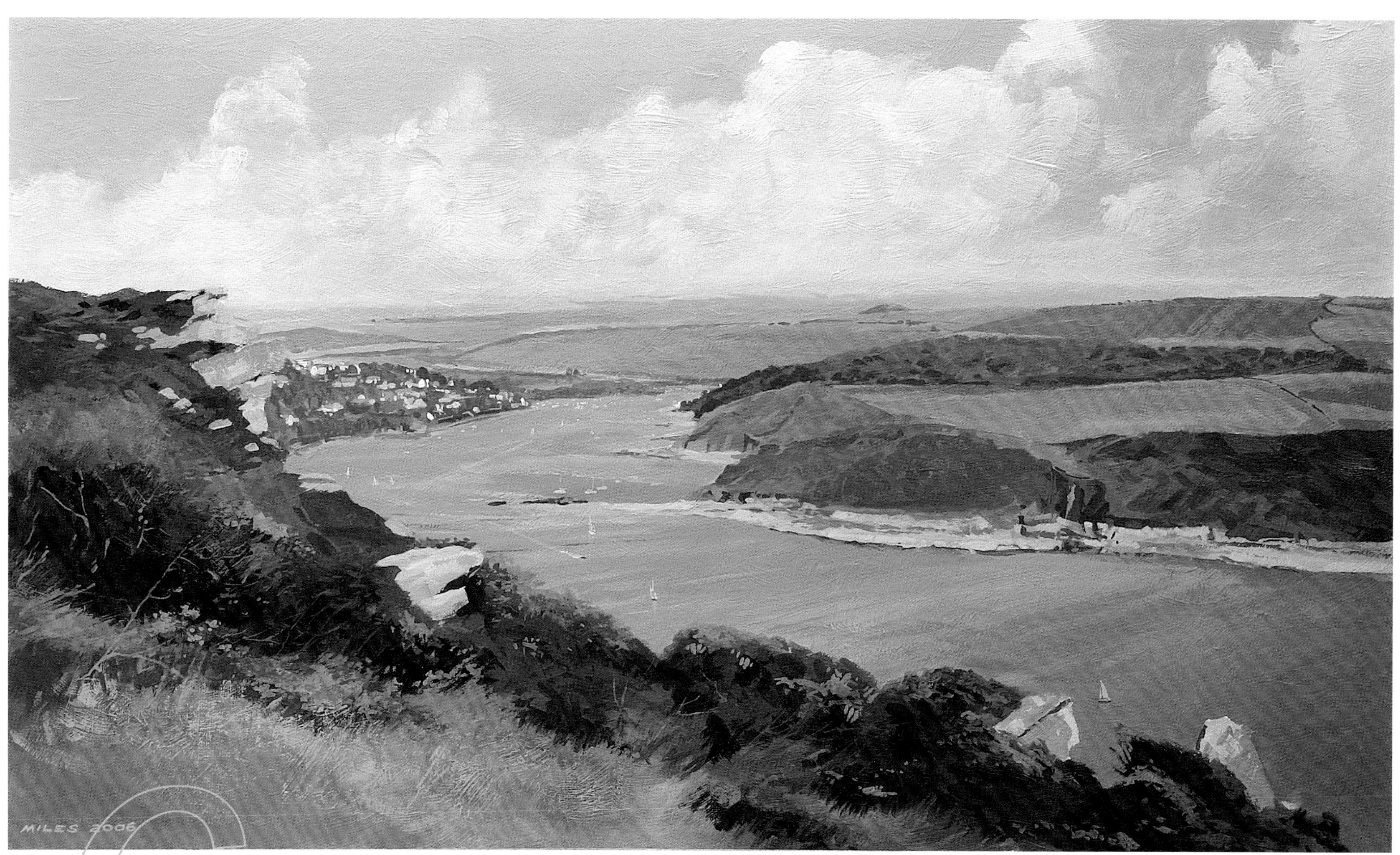


# 6 NORTH SANDS TO BOLBERRY DOWN

▲ **The Estuary from Sharp Tor**

Sharp Tor, overlooking Salcombe Harbour is the highest point along the South Hams coastline. In early summer with the gorse in bloom and banks of high cumulus rising above Dartmoor, this view epitomises the essence of the South Hams.

▲ **Stairhole Bay**

The final resting place of the four masted barque 'Herzogin Cecilie' the last of the tea clippers. The rock formation in the foreground typifies the character of the cliffs along this stretch of the coast.

▲ **The Signal Tower - Middle Soar**

This isolated squat stone building standing in the fields at Middle Soar was once the signal tower at the head of one of the runways of RAF Bolt Head, forming part of the defences of this WWII airfield.

## THE COASTLINE

There is a sharp climb in elevation from Salcombe out towards Bolt Head reaching 430ft at Sharp Tor, the highest point along the South Hams coast. The wooded hills with their secluded houses surrounding the sandy bays of North and South Sands, rise to a high plateau that drops away to The Rags and the gentler slopes around Stairhole Bay.

At the foot of Bolt Head, the tidal waters eddy around the Mew Stone and Little Mew Stone and at times storm swells bring waves crashing against the ramparts of the high cliffs that link Bolt Head and Bolt Tail. These Pre-Cambrian cliffs were raised by violent vulcanic action. Sedimentary rocks were subjected to extreme temperatures and enormous pressures and then flattened and compressed into hard schist. Due to constant erosion by wind, rain and sea they splinter and crack along their fault lines, creating tors and large square blocks and boulders. Rock shards have been put to good use in the extensive dry stone walls that divide the fields on The Warren and the slopes of Off Cove.

The only break in these impressive cliffs are the two valleys that converge at Soar Mill Cove, its sandy beach protected by the Ham Stone and its underlying reef.

## ACCESSIBLE BEACHES AND COVES

### 1. North Sands

(Access Level 1)

This is the first beach that you come to walking or driving south from Salcombe along the estuary. It is a large expanse of flat

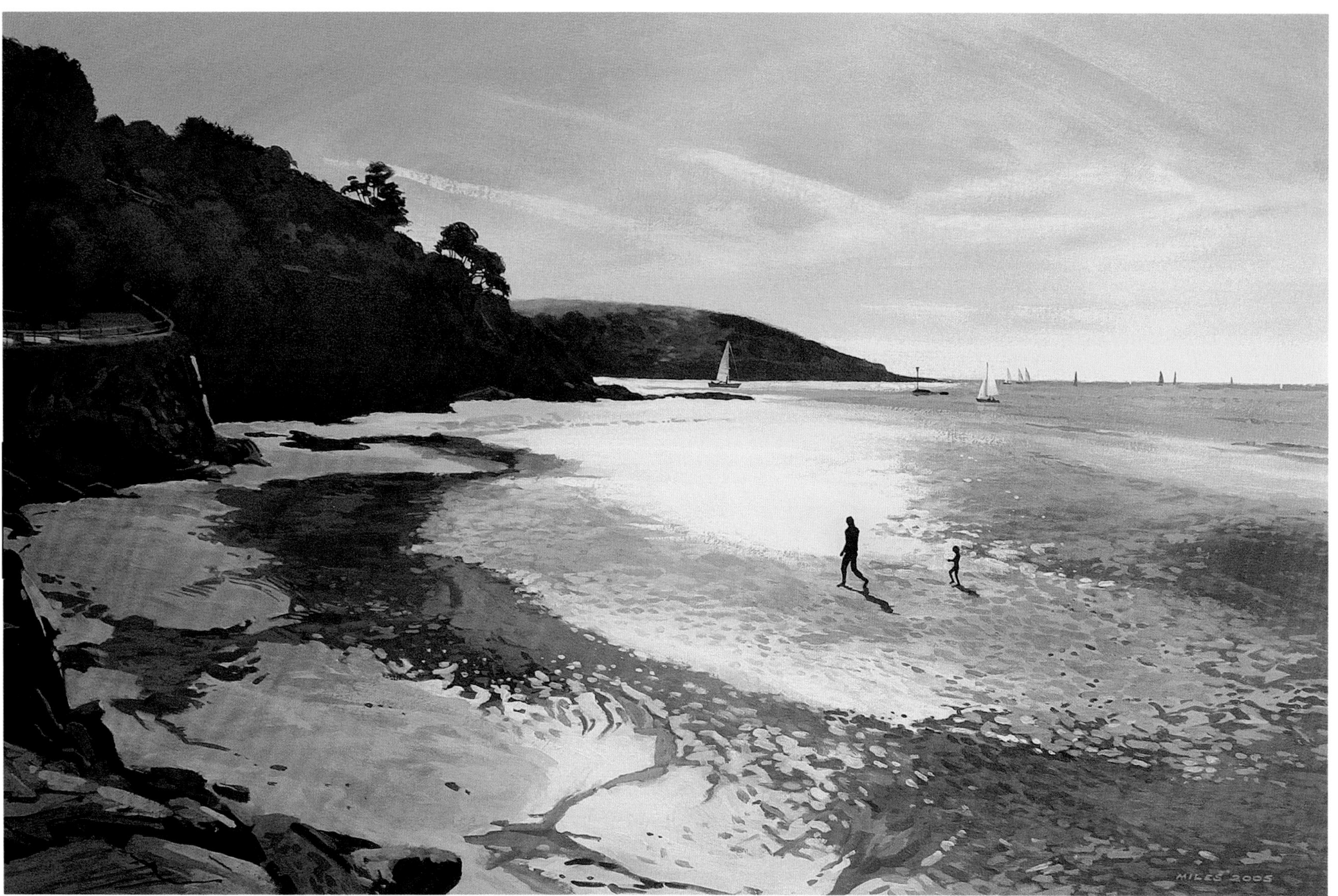


**North Sands** ▲

The sandy bays along the estuary are very attractive but leave very little beach at high tide. North Sands has adequate parking and as the sea recedes a wide expanse of sand is exposed. At low water during spring tides, you can walk out to the water's edge to get a close look at Fort Charles.

Fort Charles

**Fort Charles**

Fort Charles, that stands high on the rocks to the left of North Sands beach, adds historical interest and these ruins are accessible at low water. Built originally as Salcombe Castle to protect the mouth of Kingsbridge Estuary, it was renovated and re-named in 1643 and defended by Royalists against the Roundheads of Oliver Cromwell during the English Civil War.

sand at low tide with a small stream flowing across the beach. At high tide the sea comes right up to the sea wall and no beach remains, so it is always worthwhile checking the tide tables if you are planning a long stay with children.

There are public toilets and a large pay-and-display car park. The beach is separated from the car park by the coast road but a pavement runs behind the sea wall and there is a ramp that slopes down to the beach opposite the car park.

Refreshments are available from the Winking Prawn which is open 7 days per week between Easter and October and advertises itself as a waterfront brasserie.

Although close to the town, North Sands maintains a rustic atmosphere, enclosed by attractive wooded hillsides and backed by meadows leading up the valley behind.

Dogs are allowed on the beach.

### 2. South Sands

(Access Level 1)

South Sands is separated from North Sands by a high wooded ridge and the two bays are linked by a twisting, narrow coast road bordered by stone walls with passing places. It winds its way over the top and descends through the trees to this beautiful cove.

There is one draw back in that there is very limited car parking. A few places are available to non-residents at the Tides Reach Hotel car and caravan park but on sunny days it is best to get there early. An option to avoid this parking problem is to take the park-and -ride link into Salcombe and then sail along the estuary on the quaint and colourful, Salcombe - South Sands Ferry. Passengers transfer to a purpose-built sea tractor that meets the ferry in the water and then drives them up onto the beach to alight on the sand.

Salcombe - South Sands Ferry

▲ **South Sands**

Lying just inside The Bar at the entrance to Salcombe Harbour, South Sands is the most southerly beach on the estuary. A ferry boat runs a regular daily service between Salcombe and South Sands throughout the summer months.

The coast road runs along the back of the beach and then climbs the following ridge as a torturous switchback to The National Trust car park at Overbeck's House and Gardens. Although it's a long walk back from this car park to South Sands it is an option for those in good shape.

Like North Sands there is no sand remaining at high tide but there is a small raised promenade with seating to the left of the beach.

The Tides Reach Hotel is a thriving concern but the large hotel that stood directly on the beach next to the old lifeboat station is empty and will most likely be converted to apartments. However there is a shop and beach café in the lifeboat station above the slipway selling ice creams, tea, coffee and other refreshments. Watersports fanatics can hire surfboards, kayaks and catamarans.

There are public toilets and a public telephone in front of the car park.

No dogs are allowed on the beach in summer.

### 3. Stairhole Cove

(Access Level 3)

Stairhole Cove was not accessible to hikers in recent times due to a rock fall at the head of the tiny ravine that had swept away the lowest section of the path. This has been remedied by The National Trust which has built a metal stairway to bridge the gap.

Access to the cove is over a stile below the convergence of footpaths at Stairhole Bottom. A grass path turns back on itself into the ravine. At high tide the sea rushes up to the end of this gully but at low water

▲ **Soar Mill Cove**

This superb sandy beach at the end of an attractive valley is flanked on both sides by high cliffs. The rock formation in the centre of the painting is called The Priest. The small island is the Ham Stone

a beach of sand opens up between the rock ledges offering a secluded spot for swimming and sun bathing. Take care not to be cut off by the rising tide.

**4. Soar Mill Cove**

(Access Level 2)

This beautiful cove is quite remote, the easiest access being from a small pay car park just above the Soar Mill Cove Hotel. There is a footpath down the valley to the beach. You can also walk the coastal path from The National Trust car park on Bolberry Down.

A small stream trickles down the valley and cascades onto the beach under a wooden footbridge and there is a concrete slipway. The beach is fine sand bordered by rocks and boulders and the high buttresses and rocky outcrops give shelter from most winds. The cove faces due south and catches the sun all day long.

The most prominent feature of Soar Mill Cove is the Ham Stone, the tip of a reef that lies just offshore.

**Soar Mill Cove Hotel**

A guest house was founded in Soar Mill Cove in 1925. The building for this guest house was originally used as a cinema for the Devonport naval base. It was transported to Rew and became a temporary officer's mess for RAF Bolt Head before being set in its final location in the valley above the cove. It was completely refurbished in 1978 and opened as the Soar Mill Cove Hotel in 1979.

## WALK 11 BOLT HEAD

**Distance** **3¾ miles**
**Time** **2½ hours**
**Grade** **2**

The walk starts at The National Trust car park at East Soar. **(A)**

**RAF Bolt Head**

The car park stands at what used to be the intersection of the two runways of RAF Bolt Head, a WWII airfield. It was established in 1940, strategically placed for fighters to escort bombers on their sorties into France. It was also a base for amphibious aircraft for reconnaissance and air sea rescue operations. A plaque in the corner of the car park shows the layout of the aerodrome and explains its history.

To the left of the farm track is a low concrete building with a mast. This was originally built as a radar station with a semi-submerged bunker. In the 1950s it was upgraded to higher peacetime standards and during the Cold War it was designated a regional seat of government in the event of a nuclear attack from the Soviet Union. The airfield is still occasionally used by private light aircraft as can be seen by the wind sock next to the building, however, the grass air strip is on a different alignment to the old wartime runways.

You leave the car park and enter The National Trust land of East Soar Farm along a farm track in the direction of Sharp Tor.

The farm track turns right and you pass a footpath that crosses the fields to your left to Overbecks and Salcombe but keep straight on to East Soar Farm. Enter the farmyard passing the farmhouse and barns to your right and walk out to the fence and gate beyond the buildings. **(B)** A signpost here shows

Sharp Tor ¾ mile. Pass through the kissing gate and turn right towards a second gate at the bottom right-hand corner of the field and continue straight on. Keep following the signposts to Sharp Tor. When you eventually break through bordering gorse bushes into an open field turn right until you come to a stile. Turn left along the path that wends its way along the escarpment above Stairhole Bay.

At Sharp Tor **(C)** there is a seat where you can rest and enjoy the magnificent views of Salcombe Harbour and Kingsbridge Estuary on the one side, and the coastline out to Prawle Point on the other.

**Sharp Tor**

A compass rose mounted on a pedestal on Sharp Tor gives various bearings and distances to well known places such as Prawle Point 3 miles, the Needles-Isle of White 101 miles, Cherborg 103 miles and Lizard Point 65 miles.

Take the high footpath walking towards Overbecks and Salcombe. Go through a kissing gate and carry on past an Ordnance Survey triangulation point on your left. This path gives ever changing vistas of the estuary. At one place a swathe has been cut through the shrubs and bracken so that you can walk out to enjoy an excellent panoramic view of Salcombe. Portlemouth Down stretches away across the opposite ridge. You are standing above The Bar, a submerged sandbank at the mouth of the estuary.

You come to a flight of steps that drop down under the over-reaching branches of a tree. At the bottom turn right into a wide stone

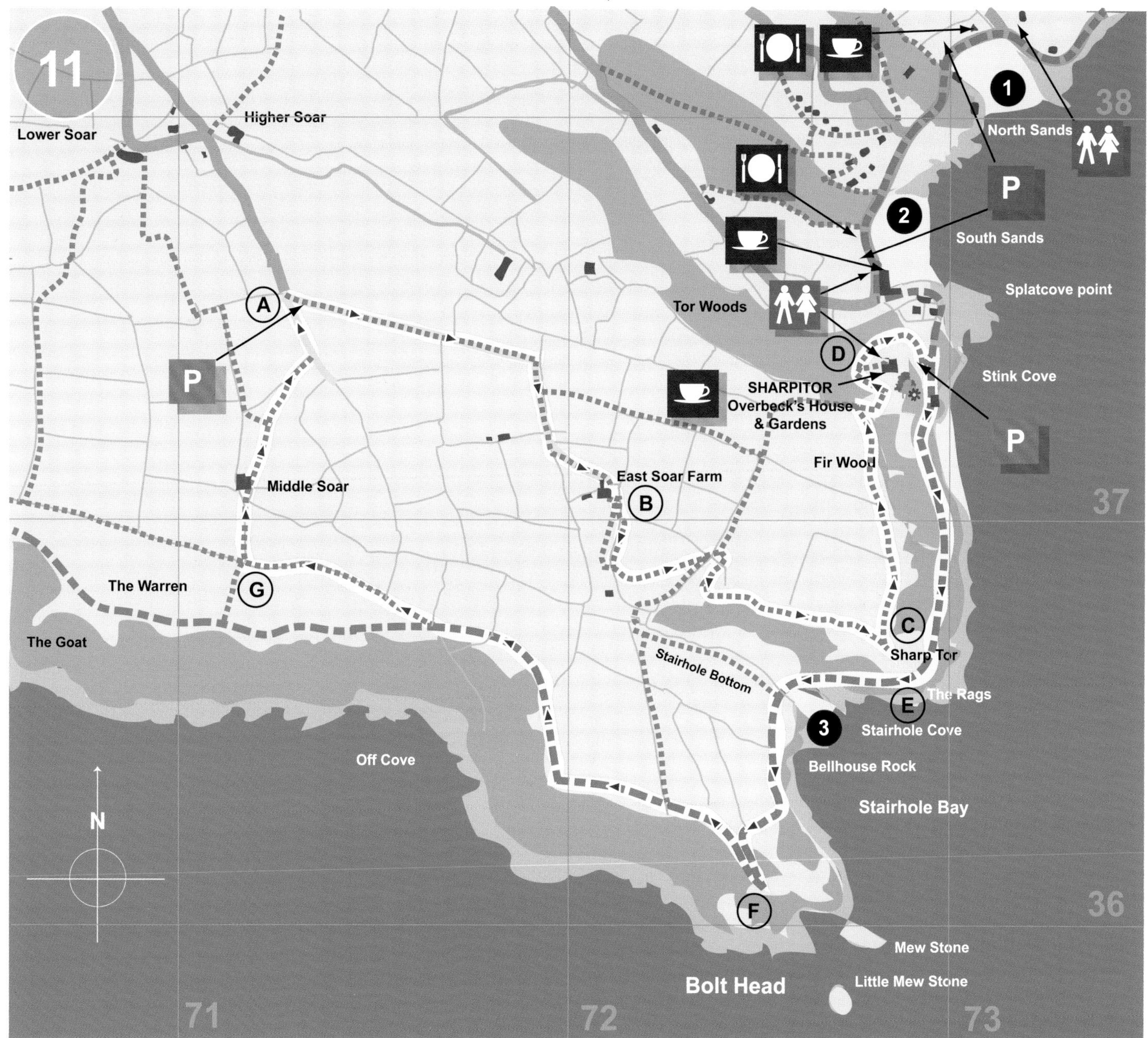

Overbeck's House and Gardens

**Overbeck's House and Gardens**

Overbeck's House and Gardens are the property of The National Trust. This was the home of the eccentric scientist and inventor Otto Overbeck who lived there from 1928 until 1937. His collection of curios includes nautical artefacts, local maritime and natural history exhibits, and two unusual contraptions. One is a 'Polyphon', an early musical juke box and the other an electrical 'Rejuvenator' which was his own invention.

The subtropical gardens surrounding the house are a series of enclosures and terraces, their borders filled with exotic sub-tropical plants.

Overbeck's has an excellent tearoom which is open throughout the summer, offering fresh cut sandwiches and home-made cakes. It should be noted that the toilets are only available when the house is open between April and October.

**The Bar**

The Salcombe Bar is thought to have been the inspiration for Tennyson's famous poem "Crossing the Bar". In 1916 Salcombe Lifeboat lost 13 of its 15 crew crossing this same bar during a raging storm, a tragedy far removed from Tennyson's romantic notion.

Beyond the Bar

track keeping to the signs for Overbecks and Salcombe. This wide stone path bears left and over the wall of the ornamental gardens you see the distinctive domed turret on the roof of the Edwardian mansion of Overbecks. **(D)**

Leaving the house and gardens go down the tarmac driveway to the junction with the coastal path and turn right. This path starts as a wide gravel driveway beyond which the track begins to climb to a wide kissing gate. This lower path leads back out to Stairhole Bay which comes into view at the top of rough stone steps cut through a massive buttress under Sharp Tor. This is The Rags, a spine of jagged rock that drops from Sharp Tor to the sea. Its contours are etched with fissures and crags. On the other side of The Rags the path turns right and is protected by a fence and wall as a safety measure against the sheer drop to the deep water swirling at the base of the cliff. From here you have an excellent view of Stairhole Bay. **(E)**

It is common to see dive boats anchored in the bay as divers explore the remains of the shallow wreck of the 'Herzogin Cecilie'

The rough hewn footpath slopes down to Stairhole Bottom where you pass through a gate and step over a stone bridge spanning a brook. A signpost shows the way to Bolt Head and you start a steady climb towards the tors above. Just when you think you have reached the summit, yet another ridge comes into view. The last stretch is of course the steepest but eventually you reach the grassy area at the crown of Bolt Head. **(F)** Here you see the ruins of a concrete WWII observation post built into the rock. Rounding the corner, the way ahead is up the grass slope between rock outcrops to a far signpost on the skyline, where you will find a gate set in a stone wall.

**'Herzogin Cecilie' stranded inside the Ham Stone.**

**Herzogin Cecilie**

The "Duchess" was the nickname given to the tea clipper 'Herzogin Cecilie', a magnificent four masted steel barque that won the Australian grain race 8 times in succession. She ran aground on the Ham Stone reef outside Soar Mill Cove during a storm in January 1937. She was re-floated after 14 days and towed to Stairhole Bay, not being allowed into Salcombe Harbour for fear that the rotting cargo might cause an epidemic. The swelling of the grain in her holds finally burst the decks and storms broke her up. Although they attempted to dismantle the ship for scrap her remains are partially buried in the sands of the bay.

From the gate, the way is signposted 2½ miles to Soar Mill Cove. The path skirts around Off Cove and after passing through two more gates you break away from the coastal path and bear right to Middle Soar along the line of a long drystone wall. This area is known as The Warren. **(G)**

Turn right through a gate signposted to Malborough taking the footpath that leads to a group of strange farm buildings with exposed gables. As you approach this desolate farmhouse there is a beautiful view down the valley to the right that opens out to frame Prawle Point.

After the farmhouse go straight ahead across the field until you reach the hedgerow and a gate opening out into a lane. Turn left and the East Soar car park is 100 yards on the right.

## WALK 12 SOAR MILL COVE

**Distance** **3¼ miles**
**Time** **2 hours**
**Grade** **2**

The walk starts from The National Trust car park on Bolberry Down. **(A)**

Take the coastal path towards Soar Mill Cove that drops down from the east side of the car park to a gate. 30 yards beyond there is a signpost to the left and a second gate that opens into the fields of South Down Farm. The footpath keeps to the top boundary of the field and gradually curves away to the right into the valley down towards Soar Mill Cove. A post waymarker points the way past rock outcrops and a line of standing stones.

To reach South Down Farm leave the valley and take the footpath rising to the left through bracken and gorse, signed Malborough 1½ miles. You cross a brook and as you gain height up the path Soar Mill Cove comes into view. The path gets steeper as you approach a farm gate beyond which it runs between high banks restricting the view. The path ends at a

Malborough
South Down Farm
Bolberry Down
Upper Soar
Middle Soar
SOAR MILL COVE
The Goat
Ham Stone
Steeple Cove
12

**South Down Farm**

South Down Farm was purchased by The National Trust in 1998 and in the same year the farmer joined the Countryside Stewardship Scheme that encourages the enhancement and conservation of the English landscape, its wildlife and history. Of the 446 acres, 180 acres is grassland and 160 acres arable land, and the rest is coastal strip above the cliffs. The farm specialises in the growing and marketing of high quality seed for garden birds. In winter the fields are left as stubble as a natural feeding ground for the local birds. In the summer months you can expect to see fields of sunflowers, millet, canary grass, linseed, oil seed rape and wheat. The farm is a haven for wild birds and several pairs of rare cirl buntings are resident as well as a large number of skylarks.

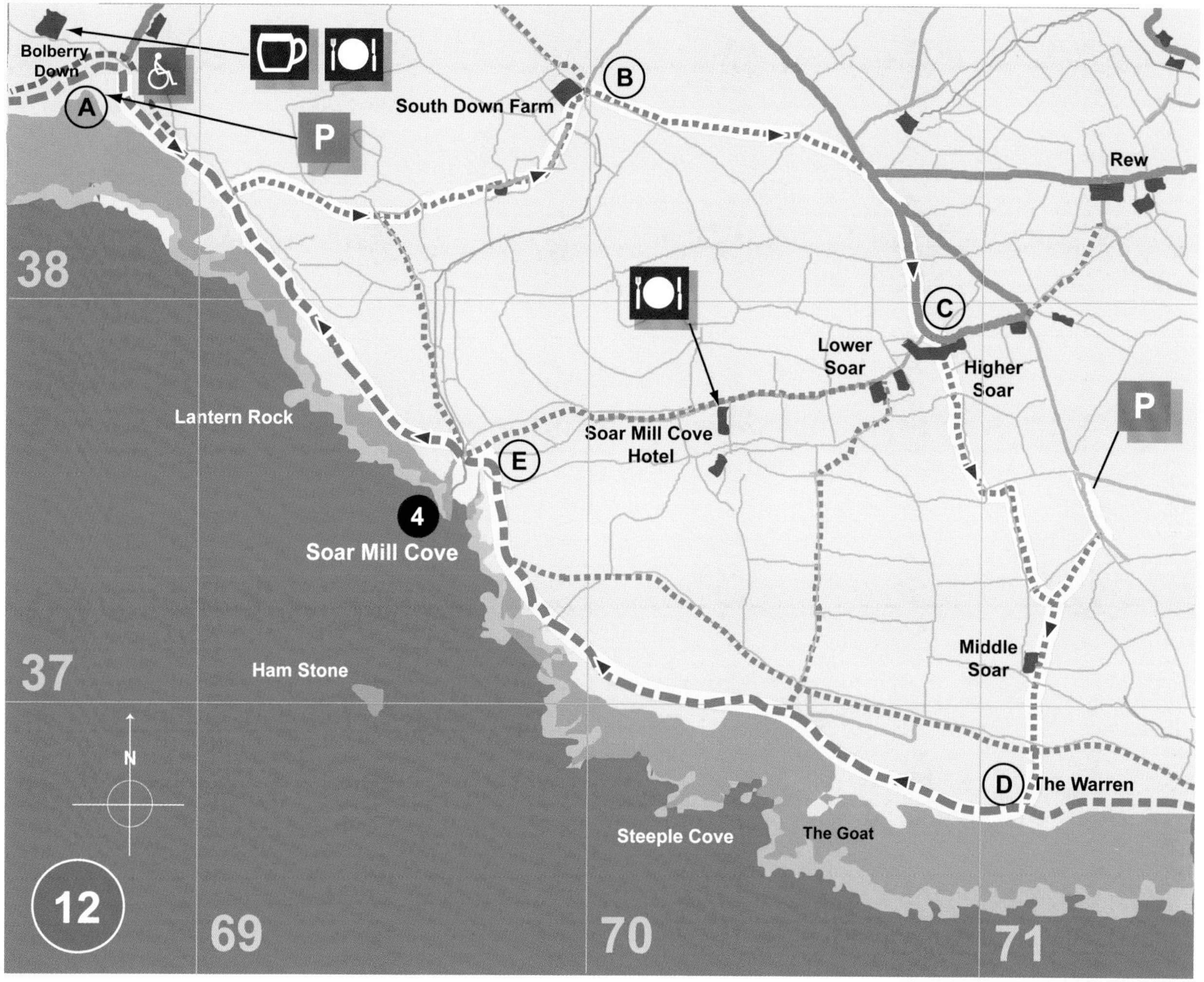

tarmac turning area in front of the entrance to Ham Stone Cottage and you follow this long driveway passed other cottages up to the farmhouse and tastefully converted barns of South Down Farm. **(B)**

The road runs through the middle of the farm complex and out into the residents car park. Opposite and to the right of the two pillars at the entrance to the farm there is a stone stile. Over the stile a wide grass farm track goes along the lower edge of the field and as the hedgerow gradually thins you get views out to sea. The most notable feature of the coastline from here is the rocky tor that seems to teeter on a plinth to the left of Soar Mill Cove.

You are directed to cross diagonally over the field between the crops. Care should be taken to stick to the path and dogs should be put on a lead to avoid any crop damage. At the top of the field the spire of Malborough church stands out high on the ridge to the left.

The path continues across the next field and once over the stile, a set of wooden steps helps you down the steep bank into a lane. At this intersection you take the road to Soar.

Walk up to Sun Park caravan and camping site and to the triangle of grass at the road junction. **(C)** To reach the next footpath look

◄ **Bolberry Down**

The National Trust car park on Bolberry Down is an excellent base for walking the coastal path between Bolt Head and Bolt Tail. This painting depicts the path as it runs eastwards from the car park towards Soar Mill Cove. The furthest headland is The Goat.

**Lower Soar**

for the line of four garages to the left of the stone cottages facing you, where you will find a signpost to the coastal path. Pass through a gate and cross the meadow to another gate in the hedgerow directly opposite. The footpath then hugs the left-hand side of the next field as it climbs up to the crest of the ridge. The stubby Signal Tower from the old airfield is a distinct landmark and you are now in Middle Soar. Exit the field and turn left.

After 20 yards the path turns unexpectedly right between the crops and crosses two fields separated by a stile. This comes out to a farm track and you turn right towards some farm buildings. This short section of the walk shares part of the route with Walk 11 and you pass the strange, remote farm house backed by dilapidated barns with exposed gables. Beyond the farmhouse, at the gate in the stone wall, go straight ahead across The Warren to the coastal path. **(D)** At the cliff edge turn right heading towards Soar Mill Cove and Bolberry Down.

Take a short stroll out to The Goat for impressive views of the coastline in both directions. In a few places the rock faces drop several hundred feet shear into the sea, but mostly rough grass, gorse and bracken covered slopes run down between rocky outcrops that end in jagged sea cliffs. You come to a footpath to Malborough and Lower Soar. This is shown on the walking map as a shorter alternative route by-passing the extended walk out to The Warren.

Soar Mill Cove comes suddenly in to view as the coast path swings left and then right around a rock formation. The path falls steeply down the grass slope to the cove. If you have packed a swimming costume and towel in your rucksack then now is the time to take a well earned dip.

On leaving the cove the footpath splits. For the energetic the coastal path to the left is a stiff climb to the top. For those feeling a little tardy after the walk, the lower path up the valley is a steady climb but not so demanding. Either way, this is the last leg back to Bolberry Down.

# 7 BOLBERRY DOWN TO AVON MOUTH

▲ **Bolt Tail**

Looking westward from Bolberry Down you have the grand sweep of Bigbury Bay. On a clear day the line of the coast can be traced beyond Burgh Island as far west as the Great Mew Stone marking the entrance to Plymouth Sound.

**Girl Jean - Hope Cove** ▲

The villages of Inner Hope and Outer Hope, separated by a high ridge, lie in two parallel valleys that run down to the shores of Hope Cove. Villagers originally made their livelihoods from fishing, but tales of smuggling and plundering of shipwrecks abound. The history of this beautiful cove is well chronicled and records go back to 1281. The site of an ancient fortification on the headland of Bolt Tail dates from an earlier time.

**Perilously Close - Shippen Rock** ►

The seabed along the entire coast of the South Hams is strewn with shipwrecks from down the ages. They are testimony as to how treacherous this rugged coastline is to shipping when storms rage.

## THE COASTLINE

The high, scalloped cliffs at Bolberry Down slope gradually away towards Bolt Tail, denoting the southerly tip of Bigbury Bay, but there is no opportunity to walk along the shoreline until you reach Harbour Beach at Hope Cove. At the base of these cliffs are a number of small bays where sand and boulders are exposed at low water, but they are completely inaccessible. This stretch of the shore under these towering cliffs is a somewhat perilous place, with shallow rock ledges shelving to deeper waters that are subject to strong currents. These tidal races stream eastwards on the flood tide, accelerating as they flow around Bolt Tail.

From Hope Cove to the mouth of the River Avon the terrain softens to rolling downs and sand dunes. The sandy beaches enjoy the relative shelter of Bigbury Bay making them suitable for bathing and water sports.

## ACCESSIBLE BEACHES AND COVES

### 1. Harbour Beach.

(Access Level 1)

This sandy beach spreads across the whole width of Hope Cove at low water. At Outer Hope it is bounded by a sea wall that provides shelter for small boats hauled up onto the dry sand above the high water line. At the opposite end of the beach at Inner Hope a stone slipway, that once served the local lifeboat station, now provides a boat launching facility for visiting yachtsmen and divers.

At high tide the beach almost disappears and all that remains is an area of sand at Outer Hope. At low water, parallel ridges of rock are exposed but the wide expanse of firm sand provides a wonderful playground for ball games. The sand slopes gently into the sea giving safe bathing conditions.

This beach is the main venue for the festivities of "Hope Cove Weekend" held each year over the Summer Bank Holiday.

There are public toilets close at hand and a kiosk, cafés, pub and village shop that cater for the needs of a day at the seaside.

Dogs are permitted on the beach all year round but must be on the lead.

### 2. Mouthwell Beach.

(Access Level 1)

The village square of Outer Hope overlooks this small sand and rock beach that is easily reached by a wide ramp. A freshwater stream cascades down the face of a high stone wall at the back of the beach and its course down to the sea is interrupted on most summer days by the construction of dams and waterways by enthusiastic children.

Another attraction is the large number of rock pools exposed by the receding tide that reveal a wealth of marine life. The beach provides safe bathing but when the sea is rough, care should be taken to avoid the rock ledges.

There is a large pay car park immediately behind the beach and the local pub, village shop and cafés are arranged around the square.

Dogs are not allowed on this beach.

**Facing the Storm - Mouthwell Beach** ▲

There is a lot to be said for exploring the South Hams coastline on warm, balmy days in spring and summer but there is also something special about wrapping up warm in the right clothing and going out to face the storm in winter.

### 3. Beacon Beach.

(Access Level 4)

This is well liked by people with small boats that sail round from Hope Cove to enjoy its remote quietness. It can be approached from Mouthwell Beach during low water spring tides, by clambering over the rocks. For the fit and agile there is a steep, zigzag track that enables you to scale the 120ft high cliff face from the coastal path above. This is not for the feint hearted. If you are contemplating making this descent, the beach can be best surveyed from the cliff top at Beacon Point.

The head of the cliff path can be found at the southern end of the beach close to the kissing gate at Woolman Point. The beach is sand and gravel and shelves steeply away from the cliff base. A strip of beach remains at high water and at low water a narrow channel of sand runs out from the middle of the beach between rock gulleys. In calm conditions this is a great place for snorkelling.

The climb back to the coastal path is very strenuous and it is strongly recommended to carry everything in a rucksack leaving your hands free.

**Thurlestone Rock**

The principal feature of the beaches at Thurlestone is Thurlestone Rock, a natural stone archway made famous by that master of landscape painting J.M.W. Turner. It derives its name from the Saxon "Torlestone" meaning pierced rock. At low tide the arch stands high and dry on a broad shelf of rock ledges that stretch out into the sea.

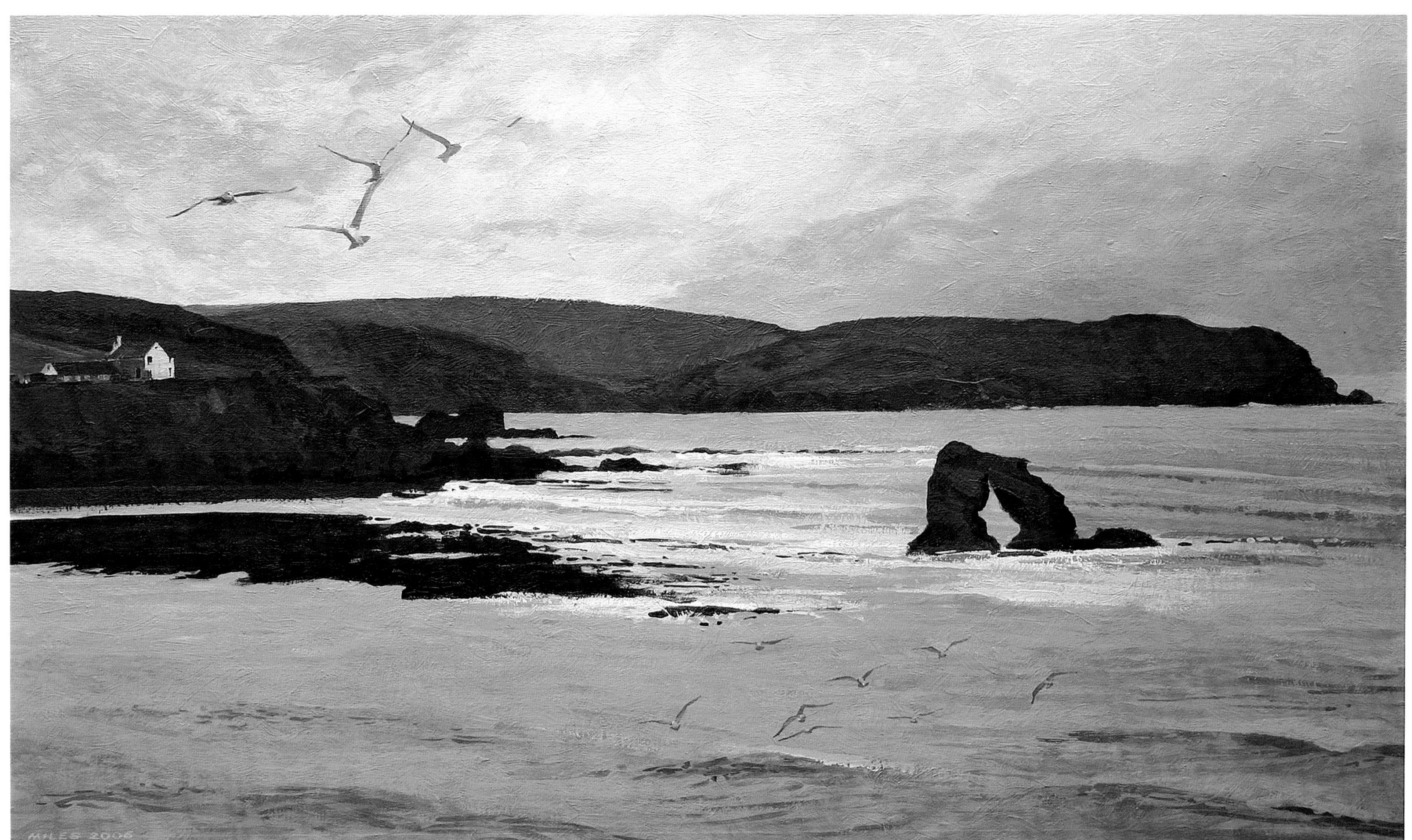


**Lowering Sky at Thurlestone Rock** ▲

The flood tide isolates this impressive stone arch once more from the foreshore; as the waves lap around its base it is left brooding in the half light.

◄ **A Fresh So'westerly - Bigbury Bay**

The beaches of South Milton and Thurlestone Sand are popular holiday destinations that offer safe bathing. The fairways and greens of Thurlestone golf course criss-cross the slopes of the far headland.

**4. South Milton and Thurlestone Sand.**

(Access Level 1)

This long beach of course sand and shingle, partly owned by The National Trust, is divided by a stream that drains from South Milton Ley. The stream is crossed by a wooden footbridge that is part of the coastal path. This is a favourite platform for birdwatchers scanning the reed beds for sightings of reed warblers, sedge warblers, bearded tits and wading birds.

There are two narrow lanes from South Milton, one on either side of the Ley that takes you down to the beaches and car parks. A single-track lane from South Huish brings you to The National Trust car park at South Milton Sand.

In the clear waters of the deep rock pools left by the ebbing tide, gobies, shrimps and crabs can be found among the fronds of bladder-wrack and kelp. Limpets, mussels, and whelks and brightly coloured anemones cling to the rocks.

Both beaches have safe bathing and during the summer months South Milton Sand is overseen by a lifeguard. There are public toilets close to the footbridge and South Milton Sand also has a refreshment kiosk and a place where you can hire water sports equipment. This beach is favoured by windsurfers and canoeists.

The two beaches are backed by sand dunes and life-buoys are prominently displayed.

Dogs are allowed but they are not encouraged on Thurlestone Sand in the summer.

**5. Leas Foot Sand.**

(Access Level 2)

Leas Foot Sand is located in front of the clubhouse of Thurlestone Golf Club, separated by the first and second fairways. This gently shelving, course sand and gravel beach, flanked by rock outcrops, offers safe bathing and is sheltered from westerly winds by Warren Point.

The golf club allows parking in its top field. If the car park is unattended then payment should be made at the clubhouse. It is a short walk to the beach.

**'Louis Sheid'**

Novice divers are introduced to wreck diving from this beach where they can explore the wreck site of the 'Louis Sheid' a Belgian ship that ran aground on the Delvers rocks at Warren Point during the blackout of WWII. After rescuing survivors from a torpedoed Dutch vessel, the captain was hugging the shore trying to escape detection by the U-Boat.

**6. Yarmer Beach.**

(Access Level 2)

The coastal path runs across the back of this fine sand beach. It can also be reached by a public footpath that crosses the golf course. A sign warns you to watch out for golfers driving over the path and to cross quickly. Leaving the beach this footpath is signposted as a right of way to Thurlestone village.

Low water exposes rock ledges along the entire length of the beach but from mid to high water, bathing conditions are good.

There is no car park in the immediate vicinity, the closest being at the golf club.

**7. Bantham Sand.**

(Access Level 1)

When the wind is in the north-east and the groundswell is coming from the south-west, Bantham Sand is the best surfing beach on the south coast. The River Avon flows out to sea, skirting around Bantham Ham, its channel separating Bantham Sand from the beach at Bigbury-on-Sea and the sand spit out to Burgh Island. The combination of sandbars, tidal flows and the swirl of the river create rip currents and for safety, bathers and surfers should stay between the red and yellow flags placed by the lifeguards. Swimming accidents on this beach are chiefly caused by these rip currents. However, provided that the safety rules are observed, swimming and body boarding can be enjoyed at all states of the tide.

The sands are constantly being sculpted by the waves and the currents. The ebbing tide leaves large pools on the beach that are perfect for toddlers to splash about in.

This large, fine sand beach is backed by Bantham Ham, an area of sand dunes covered by marram, a long, spiky grass.

There is a large car park in a field at the back of the beach with public toilets at the entrance. It is quite a long way to the Sloop Inn and village shop and tearoom in Bantham village. If you are planning to settle on the beach and stay all day then it would be a good idea to take a picnic lunch.

Dogs are not allowed during the summer.

▲ **October Reflections - Bantham Sand**

Bantham Sand is the most popular surfing beach on the South Devon coastline. When the wind and tide are just right, the shallow waters break across the sandbanks of Bigbury Bay creating long rollers. In winter it is just a great place to walk the dogs.

| | |
|---|---|
| **Distance** | **5 miles** |
| **Time** | **3 hours** |
| **Grade** | **2** |

The walk starts at The National Trust car park on Bolberry Down. **(A)**

Having parked the car, return to the car park entrance and turn left towards the Port Light Hotel.

#### Port Light Hotel

This hotel perched high on the downs has an unusual history, having been once a golf clubhouse that was converted into an RAF radar station during WWII. Bolberry Down was then an array of high masts and aerials of which only one remains.

#### Life into Landscape

Bolberry Down is the location of one of the first "Life into Landscape" projects for South Devon aimed at improving access to the countryside for people with disabilities. The paved path out to Saltern Pike and beyond is suitable for wheelchairs affording beautiful coastal views from the advantage of the 450 ft cliff tops.

The paved path ends above Broad Stone and the coastal path then continues as a stone and gravel track. The open grassland of the downs is interspersed with thickets of bracken and gorse, home to a large variety of birds and insects, while the cliffs provide nesting sites for fulmars and peregrine falcons as well as the more common gulls. Ravens can often be seen gliding and tumbling in the updraft of the cliff face.

Apart from the coastal path along the cliff edge, there are also a number of well worn paths across the grass that all converge at the far end of Bolberry Down. At Fernyhole Point you can look down into the depths of Hugh's Hole with its boulder-strewn shallows far below. The distinctive promontory of Grey Stone sits on top of the next headland, typical of the assortment of large, square rock formations and slabs that seem to balance precariously on the cliff tops along this part of the coast.

Two gates open to the next section of the coastal path. From these gates the wide sweep of Bigbury Bay is spread before you. Although the broad path is set well away from the rock faces and overhangs, these cliffs are steep and treacherous and dogs are best kept under close watch. Several have sadly met their ends chasing rabbits across the grassy slopes heedless of the danger.

As the footpath wends its way downhill towards Bolt Tail, a view of Hope Cove is revealed at the end of a broad valley to the right. When you reach the stile and five bar gate **(B)**, the wide grass track that follows the curve of the stone wall down the valley to the right leads to Inner Hope. This comes out in the middle of the old fishing village where thatched cottages are attractively grouped around a small square. This path can be taken as an alternative to the walk out to Bolt Tail, joining back with the planned route at the old lifeboat station.

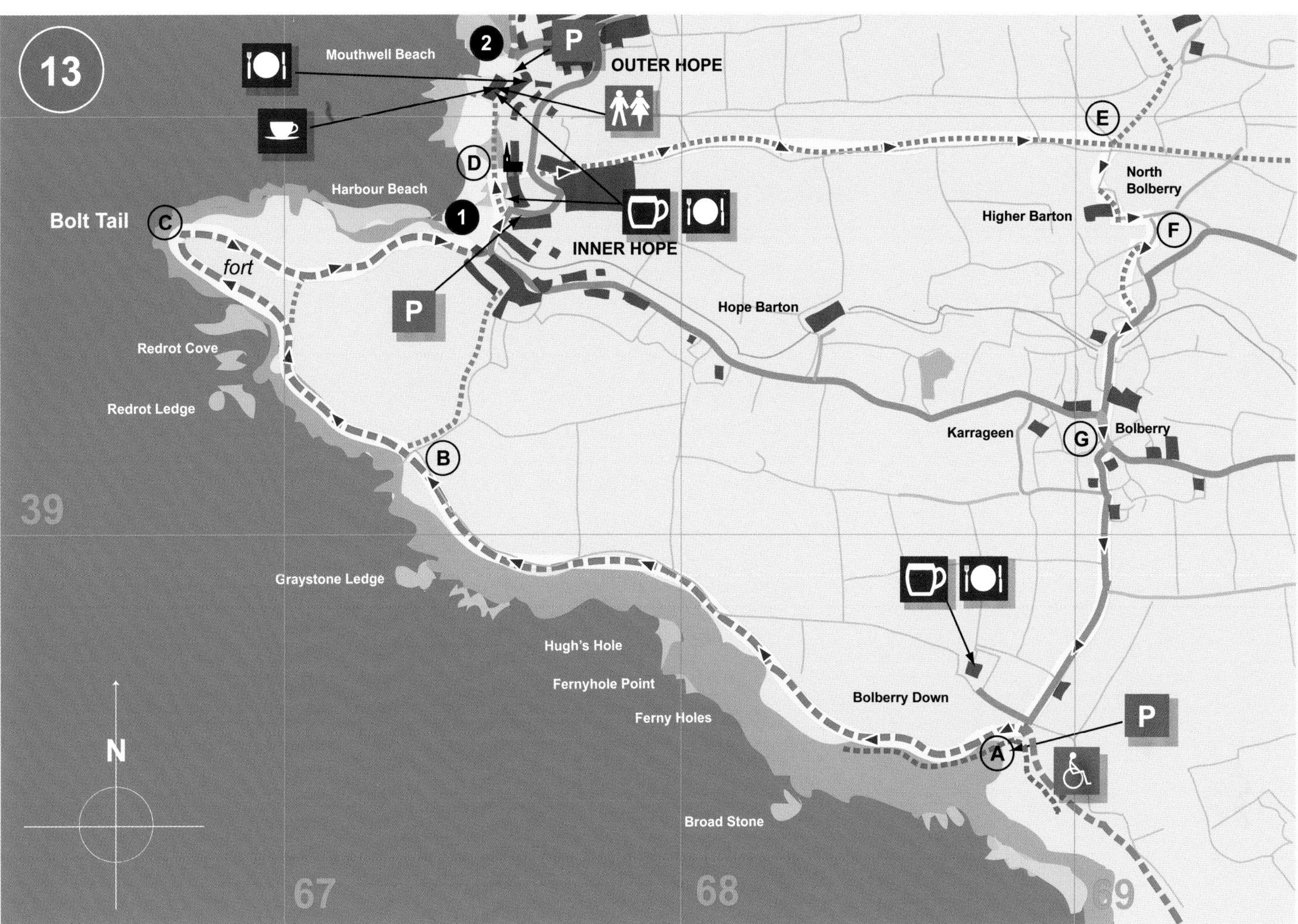



Walking directly ahead from the stile, at the top of the rise the path splits several ways across the closely cropped grass, but short waymarkers point the way along the rolling cliff top out to Bolt Tail. One of these paths bears off to the left and goes along narrow sheep trails, skirting around an impressive ravine with sheer sides that drop down into deep water. These paths merge above Redrot Cove where erosion has scoured out the high cliffs into a wide amphitheatre. Keep away from the crumbling rim where grass tussocks disguise overhangs.

A wooden bench is conveniently placed on Bolt Tail **(C)** where you can sit and watch the busy shipping in the English Channel or enjoy a glorious sunset on a mild summer evening.

**Iron Age Fort**

Beyond Redrot Cove the path rises to the stonework of an ancient Iron Age hill fortress believed to date from 700 BC, possibly home to the first inhabitants of Hope Cove, the headland having provided them with a defensive position.

#### HMS 'Ramillies'

In 1760 Bolt Tail was the site of a naval disaster when the 90 gun warship HMS 'Ramillies' was swept on to the rocks in a storm with the loss of 700 men. Parts of the wreck are still embedded in a cave at the foot of the cliffs. At the time of writing plans are in progress for a diving venture to raise one of the cannon.

Now take the footpath to Inner Hope that first descends to the floor of a grass valley and then rises and disappears into a copse on the hillside. As the path drops down through this coppice, openings between the trees and shrubs give naturally framed views of Hope Cove. Where the path divides you keep to the left eventually passing through a kissing gate and then go down a flight of steps to the slipway in front of the old lifeboat station.

#### Lifeboat Station

The plaque on the wall states that the lifeboat station was presented to the RLNI by Freemasons in 1877. The building is now adapted for the storage of fish and crabs. These days lifeboat duties are shared between the Hope Cove Coastguard Rescue Team and the RNLI Salcombe Lifeboat.

The walk continues along the pavement behind the sea wall. At high tide and with strong on-shore winds, waves crash against the wall and send spume and spray across the road and over the rooftop of the aptly named Spindrift Cottage.

As the road turns right uphill in front of the Sun Bay Hotel, turn left into the cul-de-sac signposted to Outer Hope ½ mile.

(The alternative pay-and-display car park for this walk is opposite the hotel.)

The next signpost points to Galmpton 1 mile to the right **(D)** up a steep path with steps that passes by St Clements Church set high on the embankment overlooking the harbour. This quaint church is no bigger than a village hall but once inside it is easy to imagine the gathering of fishermen and their families as they crowded into this small space to worship.

At the top of the steps cross over the road to the footpath to Galmpton. Beyond the driveway to the bungalows a farm gate opens into a field and the footpath climbs steadily for a mile along the ridge that separates Inner Hope from Outer Hope. The path follows the hedge line and there are likely to be sheep grazing in the fields as you make your way to the brow of the hill. The Holy Trinity Church at Galmpton comes into view. You pass under a telegraph line and continue up the path until you reach a gate with a stone stile set into the wall on the right-hand side. **(E)** On the other side of the gate there is a footpath to Galmpton to the left but you turn right through a five bar gate that opens to the

**Inner Hope**

footpath to Bolberry. This heads down the left-hand hedgerow and straight ahead across the valley is the Kerrigean Caravan Park. At the bottom of the field as the track bears right you turn left and climb over a stile. An arrow directs you diagonally across the meadow to a second stile. There follows a fenced path at the back of an orchard that meets the driveway of the farmhouse at Higher Barton.

Turn left along this drive and after 100 yards turn right into a farm track and walk down the hill until the signpost to Sweethearts Lane, Bolberry ¼ mile. **(F)** This is a narrow sunken footpath between high banks. It has a tendency to become overgrown in the summer months so beware of stinging nettles.

At the end of Sweethearts Lane turn right along the road to Bolberry passing beautiful country cottages and a large farm. Turn left at the T-junction with the road from Hope Cove to Malborough. **(G)** Around the bend is the lane to Bolberry Down ½ mile for the final uphill stretch back to the car park.

**Old Lifeboat Station - Inner Hope**

## WALK 14 THURLESTONE

| | |
|---|---|
| **Distance** | **6½ miles** |
| **Time** | **4 hours** |
| **Grade** | **3** |

The walk starts from The National Trust car park at South Milton Sand. **(A)**

**Special Note**

As shown on the walking map some stiles on this route have no gaps for dogs to pass through. If you take your dog on this walk it must be agile enough to spring over these obstacles.

South Milton Sand, owned by The National Trust, has public toilets and a tearoom that opens in the summer months, assuring a comfortable start to the walk. The gravel car park behind the beach looks out upon Thurlestone Rock, an arch-shaped rock formation from which the village of Thurlestone takes its name.

Leave the car park in the direction of Hope Cove. The road passes several apartment buildings after which a lane to the right takes you out to the coastal path. It is a steady climb to the top of Beacon Point. The cliffs here are continuously being eroded by winter storms and in some places the path has been re-routed away from the cliff edge and safety barriers have been put up. It is advisable to stick to the path and not be tempted to step out to the grass covered cliff edges, particularly where recent falls are evident.

After passing through a kissing gate at Woolman Point the walk turns inland up a footpath signposted to Galmpton. **(B)** This grass footpath opens out at the top into a deeply rutted farm track bordered by high banks. Occasional gateways into fields along the way offer views of Bigbury Bay, Hope Cove and Galmpton.

The farm track runs out to a road and you continue straight on. Follow the track and footpath off to the left **(C)** that drops down to the small hamlet of South Huish lying in the valley and comes out at a road junction. (It may be of interest to make a short detour to visit the ruins of the parish church of St Andrews, which is a short walk along the road to the right.) **(D)**

After visiting the church, return to the junction and follow the lane opposite the footpath around the bend to a thatched stone cottage on the left. Cross the stepping stone over a brook and take the footpath alongside the stone wall surrounding the cottage garden. The sign says "Green lane to public

The Ruins of St Andrew's Church

footpath". Climb over the stile and cross the field diagonally to the left and once over the rise make your way to the far bottom right - hand corner where a second stile brings you to a footbridge over a stream. From the right-hand corner of the next field the lane up the hill passes the cottages of Wayside and Rafters and you take the public footpath 50 yards up the road on the left. After the second stile along the footpath it leads off to the right and then begins a long climb up a steep hill over two fields to a lane at the top of the ridge. **(E)**

Climb over the stile and go left along the lane to the next footpath on the right. The trek from here to Thurlestone is an obstacle course of stone and wooden stiles, however the rewards are the views of the coast and valleys from the vantage point of the hill tops.

Walk down two fields to a road and as a check for location, to the left you will see the display board for "Horsewell Cottage and Coach House". **(F)**

Turn right and then immediately left downhill past Treadwell Farm. At the bottom of the valley the road crosses a stream and you continue walking uphill to a T-junction. Opposite is a cul-de-sac called Middle Park that leads directly to a footpath beyond the row of houses. Looking to the left along this path you can see Thurlestone Rock end-on.

Cross the next road over two stiles, walk diagonally across the field, pass through a gap in the hedge and follow the waymarkers that direct you down the next field to a country lane. **(G)** This lane takes you up to the main road into Thurlestone.

**Thurlestone**

The old village centre of Thurlestone is very attractive with thatched stone cottages, a pub and village shop crowding closely on to the narrow main street.

The tall grey slate tower of All Saints Church, at Thurlestone, is notable because of a beacon that was lit upon it to signal the sighting of the Spanish Armada as it sailed up the channel in 1588. The Village Inn incorporates timbers believed to be from the Spanish Galleon 'San Pedro' that ran aground on the Shippen Rock in Hope Cove.

**St Andrew's Church**

St Andrew's Church dates from the 13th Century but was abandoned in 1866 when a dwindling population could no longer support its upkeep and it was considered beyond repair. It was replaced by the Holy Trinity Church at Galmpton. The ruins and graveyard are preserved by Friends of Friendless Churches and are open to the public.

Turn left and walk down to the junction at Rock Hill Corner and turn right on the road to Buckland and Bantham.

Walking out of Thurlestone on the road to West Buckland the first footpath on the left is signposted Bantham ¾ mile **(H)** and as you step into the field a most impressive view opens up. This includes the River Avon flowing out to sea around Bantham Ham, Bigbury-on-Sea, Burgh Island and the high cliffs of the coastline out to the mouth of the River Erme. The distinctive white cottages of Bantham and West Buckland punctuate the green of the river valley below.

At the second field, the footpath slopes away to a stile in the bottom corner next to woodland. Further down the embankment as you walk along the edge of this wood, Burgh Island becomes the focal point of the landscape.

You cross the valley floor at the end of the wood and enter the picturesque village of Bantham on the footpath that comes out by the 14th century Sloop Inn. **(I)**

As well as the pub and restaurant at the Sloop Inn there is a tearoom at the local village shop.

The main attraction in Bantham is the

surfing beach of Bantham Sand that draws crowds of visitors at the height of summer.

Walk down through the village past the row of white painted thatched cottages, over the cattlegrid and on down the track to the large, grass car park. Make your way to the path above and to the left of the beach.

**Bantham Surf Life Saving Club**

The club was formed in 1960 to help reduce the number of drownings that occurred each year. Members of the club patrol the beach every Sunday during the summer months, the rest of the week the Bantham RNLI Beach Patrol safeguards it for bathers and surfers.

**View from the footbridge over South Milton Ley**

**South Milton Ley**

Thurlestone Marsh, South Milton Ley and South Huish Marsh are three small wetlands that lie in the shallow valley immediately behind the dunes. Canada Geese often alight on the small pond close to the car park. South Milton Ley is the most important of these wetlands as it is Devon's largest freshwater common reed bed and is designated a Site of Special Scientific Interest. It is managed in part by Devon Bird Watching and Preservation Society and supports the breeding of several species and is a roosting site for migratory birds.

You pick up the coastal path 20 yards in front of the lifeguard station. Once through the gate and stile, respect the farmer's request to stick to the perimeter of the field as you walk out to the cliff edge. Thurlestone is signposted 1 mile. It is a comfortable stroll back along the coast following the gentle contours of the cliffs and dunes. After passing Yarmer Beach, Leas Foot Sand and Thurlestone Sand you finally cross the footbridge back to South Milton Sand.

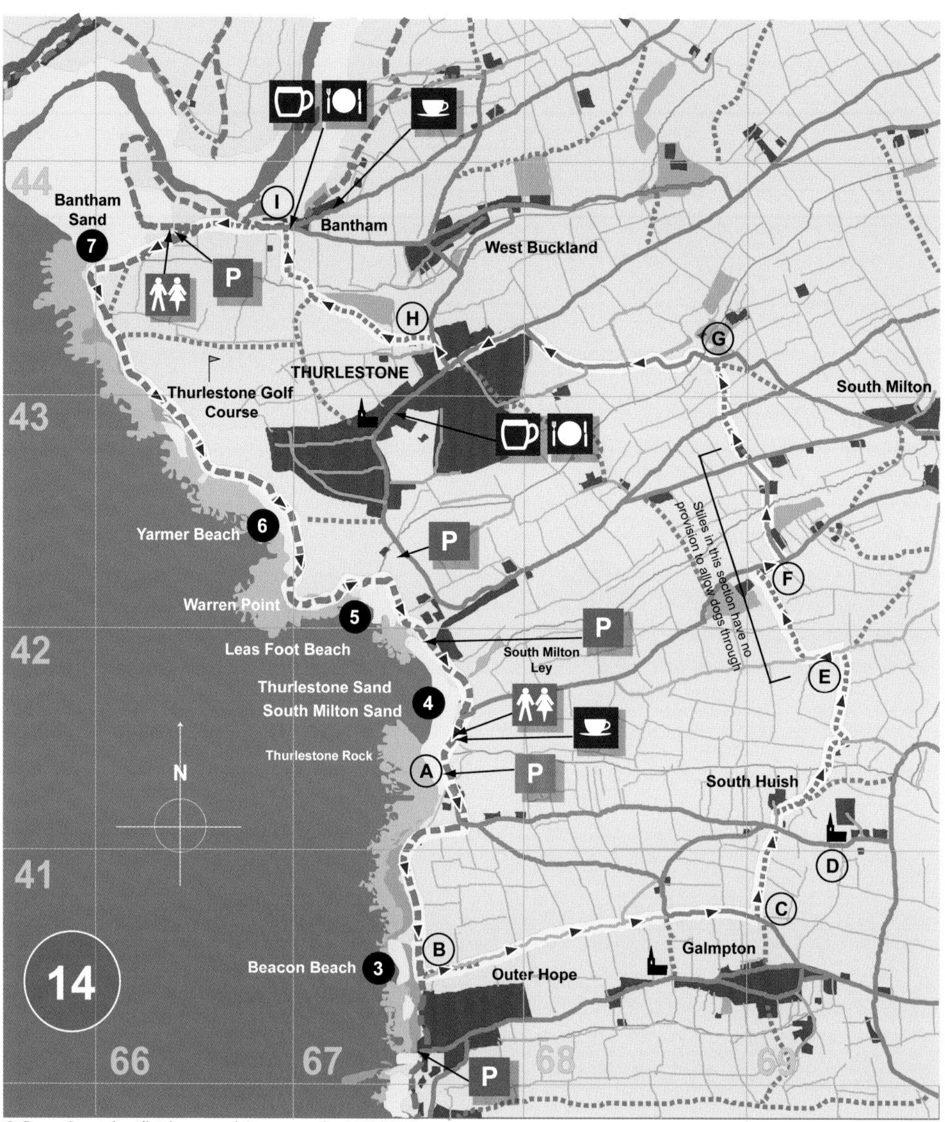

# 8 THE AVON ESTUARY

**Avon Mouth and Bantham Sand** ▲

The River Avon drains a catchment area high up on Dartmoor. It flows out to sea between Bantham and Bigbury-on-Sea. A passenger ferry crosses the river from Bantham Quay to Cockleridge Ham in the summer months, forming a vital link in the South West Coast Path. Without the ferry, hikers are obliged to take the 7 miles diversion along the Avon Estuary Trail, crossing the bridge at Aveton Gifford.

**Thatched Boathouse at Bantham**

**THE RIVER AVON**

The fresh water springs of the River Avon rise on South Dartmoor at Aune Mire, Fishlake Mire and Ryder's Mire; their combined flows feeding into the Avon Dam Reservoir to the north of South Brent. The river cascades from this remote high plateau down through steep, wooded valleys past Avonwick and Loddiswell until it reaches the head of a tidal estuary at Aveton Gifford. At low tide the river meanders lazily along this estuary between salt marshes and broad banks of mud, sand and shingle sediments until finally flowing out into Bigbury Bay across Bantham Sand, some 23 miles from its source.

The river estuary is not easily navigable because of sand bars at its mouth and only small vessels with shallow drafts are able to sail these waters. Canoes and kayaks have the river to themselves at low tide, all other craft sitting high and dry on the shoals.

A passenger ferryboat operates on the river from Bantham Quay to Cockleridge Ham during summer months from Easter to early September, between 10:00am – 11:00am and 3:00pm – 4:00 pm every day except Sundays. The A379 main road at Aveton Gifford bridges the uppermost reach of the estuary.

The only commercial enterprise on the estuary is Bigbury Bay Oysters and Mussels based at Milburn Orchard at the end of the tidal road. This shellfish farm is a family run business that produces finest quality pacific oysters in netted bags laid in the riverbed. The nutrient-rich tidal flow of seawater mixed with the fresh water of the river provides perfect conditions for oyster growing. Opportunity to taste this delicacy is provided at the Oyster Shack Restaurant just up the hill from the farm.

The river valley still presents a beautiful unspoiled environment, a tranquil rural landscape, sparsely populated with a rich variety of wildlife.

**Dinghy Sailing at Bantham** ▲

Bantham Sand is renowned as the best surfing beach in the South Hams but just up river at the village of Bantham dinghy sailing is very popular. The river in full flood sweeps in a wide arc past the small quay and boathouse that nestle under the thickly-wooded embankment. Contrary winds and tidal surges make sailing here quite challenging.

AVETON GIFFORD
Doctor's Wood
Milburn Orchard
Stiddicombe Wood
Bigbury Golf Course
BANTHAM
RIVER AVON
Ferry Crossing
Cockleridge Ham
Bantham Ham
Car Park
15
Bantham Sand

**Distance** 6½ miles
**Time** 4½ hours
**Grade** 3

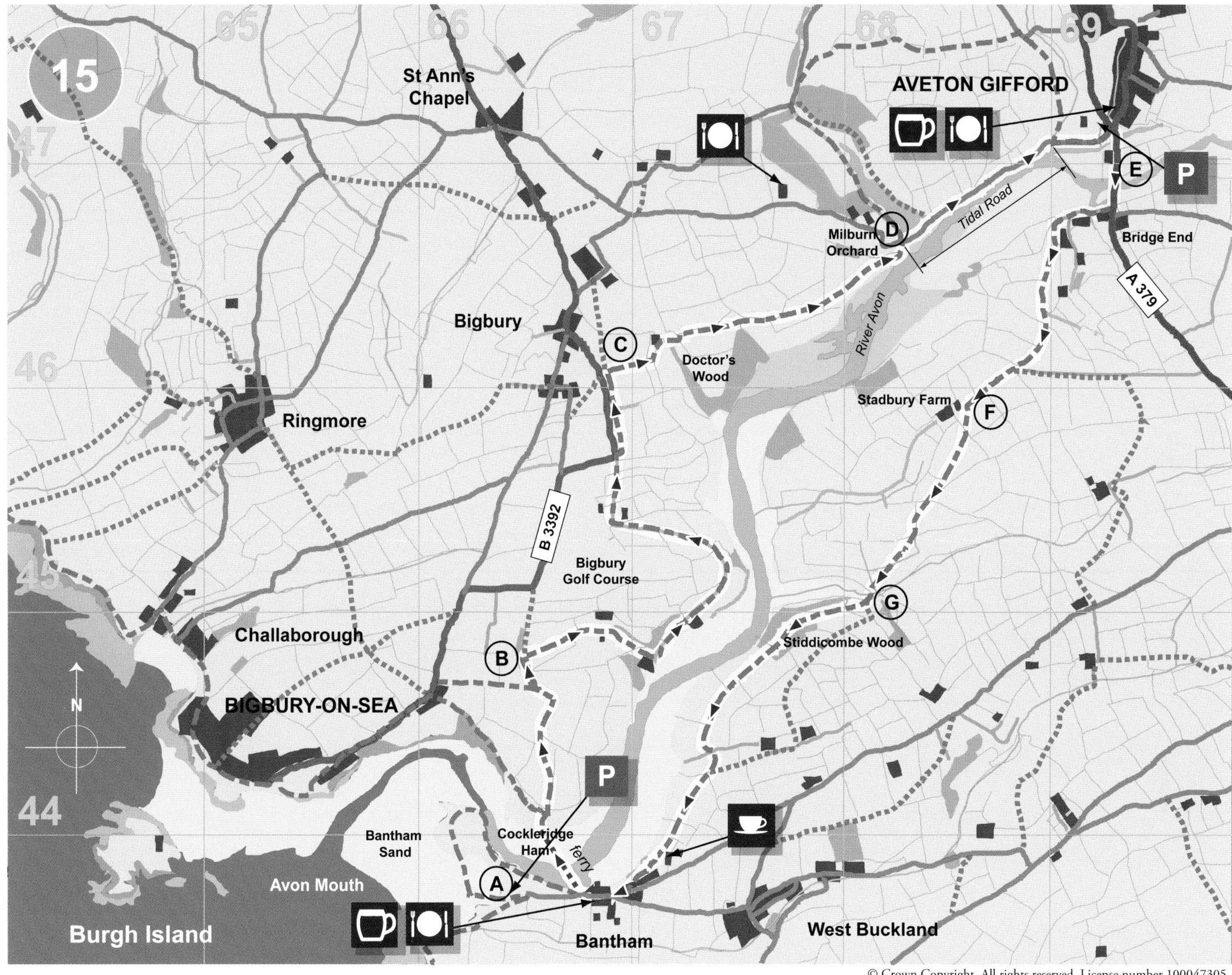



The walk starts at the pay car park in Bantham. **(A)**

Note: Because of the tidal road at the head of the estuary at Aveton Gifford, this walk has to be planned around the times of the ferry crossing at Bantham and the time of high water. The best combinations are on days when high tide falls between 6:00am and 7:00am coupled with the morning ferry crossing between 10:00am –11:00am: or alternatively days when high tide falls between 11:00am and 12:00 noon coupled with the afternoon ferry crossing between 3:00pm – 4:00pm. The tidal road floods 2 hours either side of high water and these combinations give the greatest latitude in the pace of the walk.

Exit the car park and take the lane immediately to the left sign posted "Coast path to Ferry". Depending on the state of the tide, the ferry will either depart from Bantham Quay or from the water's edge.

The ferry lands at Cockleridge Ham on the other side of the river, and once you alight make your way to the grass and scrub area above the beach and locate the signpost for the public footpath to Bigbury 1¾ miles. The footpath is a steep climb up to a stile where you can turn and admire the view of the river.

Beyond the stile the path widens as it climbs further along the side of a field turning left at the top, clearly signed by a waymarker. Now the view has widened to include Bantham Sand and Burgh Island and the houses of Bigbury-on-Sea that line up along the edge of the cliffs.

Leave the field at the top left-hand corner and continue the climb along a paved lane that enters the grounds of Bigbury Golf Course. Take time to assess the state of play and listen for shouts of "Fore!" as players tee off. It is polite and sensible to wait until the golfers signal that it is safe to walk on.

This perimeter road bears left and as you make your way further up the rise the Clubhouse appears. Keep to this road that crosses a fairway until you come to a lane to the right over a cattle grid. **(B)** This descends towards the river and a group of converted barns at the bottom. You pass an old apple orchard on the right and step past a second cattle grid through a kissing gate to enter the hamlet. After a row of garages the paved road becomes cinder at the end of which a gate opens to a wide grass track.

The path appears to split but go on down the hill through a five bar gate under an arch of trees until you step out in to a country lane where you turn left following the footpath sign. High banks with old gnarled oak trees flank the lane and apart from one small glimpse there are no views of the river until you reach a left-hand turn in the road. If you followed the recommended timing for the walk then the tide will have ebbed and the river will appear as a series of shallow channels coursing between wide sand and shingle bars. Doctor's Wood covers the slopes of the hills to the left of the bend in the river.

The lane continues to climb away from the river up the side of a valley and there are now constant views of the river through breaks in the trees and bushes. On the next bend you pass Lincombe Barn and Lincombe House and high banks once again obscure the views. It has been a long steady climb since walking down from the golf course to the river but you are now on the last furlong to the top of the hill. Here the golf course borders the road and you may see players on the fairway up on the bank to the left.

There is an opening through the hedge on the right into a field with a notice declaring "Conservation Walks". More specifically when you step into the field the permitted footpath is signed and another notice says, "This short section of permitted footpath is designed to allow you to walk off the public highway". Go over the brow of the hill keeping to the left-hand hedgerow; to the right you can see up the river valley as far as the bridge at Aveton Gifford and the houses and church spire of Bigbury are straight ahead. Pass through railings set in the next hedge and carry straight on. At a gap in the hedge to the left you are treated to a vista of the English Channel seen through a cleft in the hills.

Now take the public footpath to Milburn Orchard 1½ miles crossing the field between the crops, heading down the hill towards the river. **(C)** At the far side of the field climb the stile and enter the tunnel of trees and bushes fringing Doctor's Wood. It can become quite sticky under the trees when the run-off after rain turns part of the track into a rivulet. This water diverts down a path to the right but the walk goes straight on and breaks out of the copse at the top of the rise. The level grass track then keeps to the line of the fence above a steep grass bank that rolls down to the valley floor.

At the next stile a notice asks for dogs to be kept on the leash and this enclosed section ends at a wicket gate and water trough. Directly ahead is a wide panorama of the river as it meanders around two bends. Broad, etched mudflats, covered in green algae are exposed with small boats and larger catamarans stranded on the banks or in mid-channel. This is the part of the estuary farmed for oysters and it is quite possible to see someone with a wheelbarrow tending to the turning of the netted bags, or groups enjoying a guided tour of the oyster beds. The burbling cry of the curlew often echoes around the hills.

Crossing the next field do not get misled by well-worn sheep or cattle trails, the footpath edges down the hillside to meet with a stile in the middle of the fence.

The descent from here to Milburn Orchard is hard on the ankles as you traverse the angled slope of the fields. At the bottom where wire fences converge, a stile leads to a small meadow where you should look out for bronze statues of two deer standing among the trees. After climbing yet another stile, steps bring you down a steep bank to the riverbed and the start of the tidal road marked by wooden piles. **(D)**

Take the road up to the bridge at Aveton Gifford where the A379 crosses the estuary. The tidal road is quite narrow in places and there is often a steady stream of traffic. At the roundabout there is a free car park that could be used as an alternative starting point for this walk. (Setting off from here you are still bound by the same relationship between the ferry times and high water.)

**The Avon at Aveton Gifford** ▲

The Avon is still tidal as far up river as the bridge at Aveton Gifford. When hiking the Avon Estuary Trail you need to take the state of the tide and ferry times into consideration to avoid a lengthy diversion when the tidal road alongside the river floods at high water.

As you step out on to the bridge **(E)** you get good advise from a notice stating, "Caution. Busy Bridge. Please Take Care". Although the speed limit over the bridge is 40mph it can be unnerving when large articulated lorries are bearing down. There are permissive walkways safely tucked behind walls on the left-hand side but where the bridge crosses the water in two places, there is no pavement and you are obliged to walk in the road. Keep to single file with dogs on a short lead. At the end of the long bridge, re-cross the A379 to the no-through road at Bridge End to begin the 3½ miles trek back to Bantham along the other side of the estuary.

The lane passes Efford House and a group of converted barns before bearing left and narrowing to a grass track at the beginning of a long ½ mile arduous climb up a sunken trail. It eventually comes out into the country road to Stadbury Farm at Higher Stadbury. Disappointing news after the last uphill slog to see the signpost to Bantham still given as 3½ miles.

At the entrance to Stadbury Farm **(F)** a footpath leads off to the left through a thicket, soon merging with a grass track out to an open field. The walk follows the boundary of the next two fields and a view opens up to the sea. Above the rooftops and chimneys of Higher Stadbury to the right, Dartmoor traces the skyline. At the bottom of the second field the path turns left into a fenced off section that ends at a five bar gate.

Turn right as directed by the waymarkers along the top of the high bank above a deep wooded valley until the point that the track turns and disappears into scrub. Although there is no indication, the estuary trail goes left down the steep grass bank to the bottom of the valley. Here you pick up a waymarker and the path becomes more distinct as it runs on through the trees to a double-gated opening to a creek bed. **(G)** At the head of the creek, railway sleepers cross a brook and steps cut in the bank go up to a gate.

Turn right and head across the field to the stile at the entrance to Stiddicombe Wood. This mature woodland is a joy to walk through; it is well managed and comprises mature sycamore, beech, sweet chestnut, horse chestnut, hazel and holly. The path is well signed and on sunny days beams of light filter down through the high, leafy canopy to dapple the floor of the glade. Beyond the wood, that you leave by a kissing gate, you step back into the open spaces of fields that slope down to the banks of the river.

This is the glorious finale to the walk. From here the river is always in sight as you cross three fields separated by five bar gates and stiles. On the other side of the estuary, above the woods, the fairways and greens of Bigbury Golf Course carpet the hilltop. Directly ahead there is an expanding panorama that includes the river channel dotted with boats and groups of mute swans, the majestic sweep below Bantham, and a second bend around Ham End that draws the eye out to Bigbury Bay.

On leaving the third field the path splits and you take the right-hand fork down to a gate. Drop down into the shallow valley, cross a brook and climb up the other side to a stile. Turn right and this level farm track returns you to Bantham.

# 9 BURGH ISLAND TO THE RIVER ERME

**Bigbury Bay** ▲

There is a public footpath that crosses the hill from Thurlestone to Bantham. As it tops the ridge the walker is treated to this breathtaking panorama of Bigbury Bay, with Burgh Island shown off to its full glory set against the backdrop of high cliffs under Toby's Point, Hoist Point and The Beacon. The coast rolls on beyond the mouth of the River Erme westward to Plymouth Sound.

**The Pilchard Inn and Special Tractor**

## COASTLINE

The golden sands at the mouth of the River Avon shape the beaches of Sedgewell Cove and The Warren that separate Burgh Island from Bigbury-on-Sea. Burgh Island is the most prominent feature of the coastline between the Avon and the Erme, a focal point for holidaymakers and visitors to Bigbury-on-Sea and Challaborough, the most westerly of the coastal villages of Bigbury Bay.

Beyond Challaborough the peaks of Toby's Point, Hoist Point and The Beacon form a switchback of rolling hills, their sides plunging into deep valleys, their sheer cliffs of mica schist ending in impressive formations with great shining slabs of rock that mirror the sunlight. The coastal path follows the roller coaster contours of the cliffs along these wild and remote downs interspersed by the lovely sand and shingle beaches at Ayrmer Cove and Westcombe Beach.

Rounding The Beacon and Fernycombe Point the scene softens to the sands of the charming flooded valley of the river Erme, flanked on both sides by densely wooded hills.

## BURGH ISLAND

Burgh Island is briefly separated from Bigbury-on-Sea by 200 yards of water for about 3 hours either side of high tide.

The sands of Sedgewell Cove and The Warren merge as the sea ebbs away and once the beach has dried visitors can walk across the causeway to explore the island, or visit the quaint and historic Pilchard Inn. At high tide the hotel on the island operates a special tractor shuttle service.

The island was originally known as St Michael's Rock, named after a 14th century chapel that crowned the summit where now stands the remains of a huer's hut. The original cottage that houses the Pilchard Inn dates from the same period and there may once have been a monastery on the site of the hotel.

In the 18th century the island was renowned for harbouring smugglers and wreckers. One such notorious villain, Tom Crocker, is said to haunt the Pilchard Inn, where he spent much of his time. There is not a great deal known about him and speculations differ as to how he met his end. Some say he was shot outside the pub, whereas others claim that he was hanged.

Pilchard fishing was once extremely important to the local community and in the 19th century there were several fisherman's cottages as well as a pub on the island. The "hue and cry" from the lookout when a large shoal of pilchards was sighted would alert the fisherman to launch their boats and put to sea after their quarry, with the huer signalling semiphore directions to the boats from the top of the island using bushes or flags.

The island is best known for the large imposing art deco hotel that boasts an impressive guest list of famous people such as Agatha Christie, Noel Coward, Edward and Mrs Simpson, Winston Churchill, Amy Johnson and The Beatles. The hotel was built in 1927 and although it suffered bomb damage during WWII, successive owners have restored and renovated it, retaining the interior design of the1930s.

Burgh Island is privately owned and in recent years there has been controversy over the public right of access to the island. A submission by Bigbury Parish Council to have pathways to the summit and a circular path on the west side of the island mapped as recorded footpaths was upheld by Devon County Council in 2006. At the time of writing this order is awaiting government approval and at the moment the tracks are signed as permitted footpaths.

▲ **Burgh Island**

Once a hide-away for smugglers and wreckers, the island is now a popular tourist attraction. A special tractor ferries passengers to and fro, high and dry above the waves when the beach is covered. The art deco hotel looking like a stranded cruise ship was a favoured retreat of Agatha Christie who wrote her novels "And Then There Were None" and "Evil Under the Sun" while residing there.

**Flat Calm – Ayrmer Cove** ▲

Ayrmer Cove lies to the west of Challaborough, the two beaches separated by the headland of Toby's Point. This remote, secluded cove with its shining cliffs of mica contrasts sharply with its neighbour that bustles with families enjoying the seaside entertainment and facilities of a popular holiday park.

## ACCESSIBLE BEACHES AND COVES

### 1. Bigbury-on Sea

(Access Level 1)

Bigbury-on-Sea has benefited from the facelift it got in 1990 when the old pilchard-processing shed was replaced with an attractive apartment complex on the waterfront.

The beaches of Sedgewell Cove and The Warren combine at low water to give a long unbroken stretch of fine golden sand that wraps around the promontory of Bigbury-on-Sea. This became a Blue Flag beach in 2005 reflecting the cleanliness of the water and the quality of the amenities.

As the tide floods, the causeway to Burgh Island is swamped, and the encroaching tide eventually ushers the beach lovers and sun worshippers up the slipway and steps as the sea laps against the foreshore rocks. The sea and waves at high tide becomes the province of wind surfers and kite surfers and visitors to Burgh Island flock onto the raised platform of a purpose-built tractor to chug over the sea to the island.

There is a large pay-and-display car park above the beach connected to the sands by a steep curving ramp as well as steps. There is a beach shop, good public toilet facilities, and a café offering a wide selection of food and refreshments. In the village there is a Post Office and store. Many will choose to cross to Burgh Island for a pub lunch or a drink at the Pilchard Inn.

RNLI lifeguards are on duty between 10:00am to 6:00pm every day from 19th May to 24th September.

Dogs are allowed on Warren Beach but are

excluded from Sedgewell Cove during the summer.

### 2. Challaborough

(Access Level 1)

Challaborough is a long drive from the A379 that ends in narrow single-track roads from Bigbury or Ringmore. Car parking is restricted to about 70 spaces and it is worth considering the short walk along the cliff path around the headland from Bigbury-on-Sea to reach this beach.

The valley behind the sheltered beach is filled with the chalets and static caravans of a large holiday park and the small crescent beach of fine sand and rocks becomes crowded with families at the height of the season. It is a great beach for children, the fine sand ideally suited to building castles and there are plenty of rock pools at low water

Emergency and rescue facilities are provided by RNLI lifeguards, offering a matching service to those at Bigbury-on-Sea.

Amenities include toilets, a restaurant and bar, café and a shop.

Dogs are not allowed on the beach.

### 3. Ayrmer Cove

(Access Level 2)

This is a secluded beach of shale, shingle and sand at the head of a shallow valley of lush grass meadows running down to the sea from the village of Ringmore. A National Trust car park in Ringmore is especially provided for Ayrmer Cove and it is a pleasant and easy walk down the footpath to the beach.

The coastal path runs along a raised grass bank at the back of the cove, crossing a small wooden bridge over a stream.

A shingle ridge remains at high water but as with most remote coves it suffers from the usual litter of flotsam and plastic waste that washes up on each tide. The water recedes between rock ridges with a sandy bottom giving a good entry for swimmers. At the lowest state of the tide it is possible to clamber over the rocks and through a tunnel to the adjacent beach at Westcombe.

### 4. Westcombe Beach

(Access level 3)

Even more remote than Ayrmer Cove, Westcombe Beach is reached by a stiff climb over the high ridge that separates the two bays. This is a truly wild and spectacular cove bordered on both sides by magnificent rock formations. Lines of bedrock radiate from the base of the higher beach but lower down they burrow back into the shingle and sand so that at low water there is perfect bathing.

The coastal path descends to the back of the beach and there is a track down to this valley from Kingston following the course of a stream that flows out onto the beach.

### 5. Wonwell Beach

(Access Level 2)

This lies in the estuary of the River Erme and even at high water there remains a lovely sandy beach and safe swimming. The serious drawback is that there is only very limited parking in the narrow country lane from Kingston. A confined turning space at the end of this road provides escape if all "sensible" parking has been taken. It is a question of first-come-first-served and using common sense to avoid restricting the movement of passing vehicles.

At low water you can walk to the beach from the slipway along the flat sands of the estuary but you must take the coastal path at high tide.

## WALK 16 AYRMER COVE

**Distance** **5½ miles**
**Time** **4 hours**
**Grade** **3**

The walk starts from The National Trust car park for Aymer Cove in Ringmore. **(A)**

At the start of the footpath in the corner of the car park there is a colour plaque illustrating a shorter circular walk down to the cove and back up the valley to the village.

It is an easy 10-minute walk to the beach on a well-worn and way-marked footpath. Ayrmer Cove is the property of The National Trust and a sign asks that you avoid leaving litter, lighting fires and damaging trees or plants. Another notice could be added advising young visitors to resist the temptation to climb the rock faces. A number of rescues have had to be organised for climbers injured or stranded on the cliff ledges both here and at neighbouring Westcombe Beach.

Nearing the cove the sunken path with high hedgerows that have inhibited the views, gives way to a low stone wall bordering a grass meadow. The impressive rock formation to the right of the bay dominates the scene. On the left a grass covered hillside rises up to Toby's Point that separates Ayrmer Cove from Challaborough.

Cross the wooden footbridge spanning the stream at the back of the beach **(B)** to stone steps that begin the stiff climb over the hill to Westcombe Beach.

Once you have reached the top of this rise, looking back you are treated to a view of Burgh Island and Bigbury Bay. The path flattens out on the brow of the hill and curves round to the tip of the headland where you look down upon the lovely expanse of Westcombe Beach spread out far below. Care should be taken here since fresh earth is often

All Hallows Church - Ringmore

exposed at the edge of these cliffs as evidence of recent erosion.

There is a stile at the top of the hill to a permitted footpath returning along the ridge back to Ringmore, but you descend the hillside to Westcombe Beach, assisted by steps at the steeper places.

(The next section of the walk to Kingston is shared with Walk 17.)

Westcombe Beach is a secluded spot at the head of a valley. **(C)** Cross the footbridge over the brook that runs onto the shingle, turn right over a stile, and take the permissive footpath signposted to Kingston 2 miles. This wide path alongside the stream is a very easy walk up the valley but when you re-cross the stream at a second footbridge the path then starts to climb through a thicket up to a fork in the track. Continue on the bridleway to Kingston 1½ miles.

The track climbs among woodland and after periods of rain the deep ruts left by

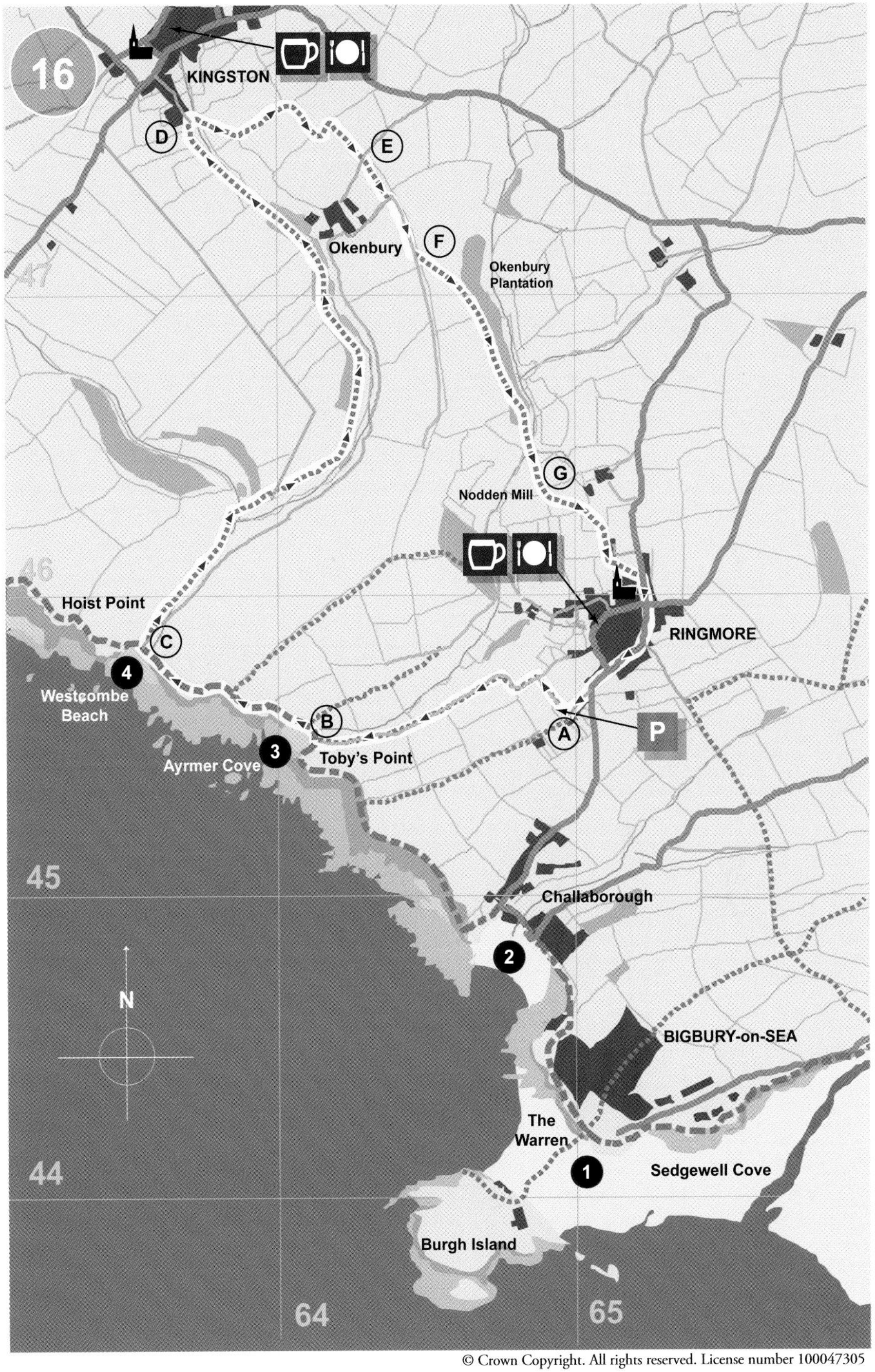

16

KINGSTON

Okenbury

Okenbury Plantation

Nodden Mill

Hoist Point

RINGMORE

Westcombe Beach

Ayrmer Cove

Toby's Point

Challaborough

BIGBURY-on-SEA

The Warren

Sedgewell Cove

Burgh Island

**Westcombe Beach.** ▲

Hoist Point towers above the rock-scarred beach of Westcombe, the grass downs rolling onward to The Beacon. Breasting the tops of these beautiful headlands wonderful vistas open out to reward the effort of the climb.

**Noddon Mill**

farm vehicles can become extremely muddy underfoot. You can hear the tinkling of the stream away to the right as it spills down the valley and as you get closer to Okenbury you pass a series of man-made ponds. At one place a small waterfall separates the pools and there is a crossing with another farm track. Further along, the mill and cottages at Okenbury can be seen through the trees reflected in the waters of a mere, the last and largest of the ponds. Okenbury is a very old medieval estate, The Manor having been mentioned in the Domesday Book. Less attractive is the Kingston Water Treatment Works at the outskirt of the village where the farm track opens out to a wide gravel road.

Upon entering Kingston you turn right in front of Walkespool Cottage with its striking white gables, following the signpost to Ringmore 1½ miles. **(D)** The public footpath goes into the cottage garden, crosses the lawn and then passes between the vegetable plot and a chicken pen. Needless to say dogs must be kept on the lead. At the end of the garden turn left to some stone steps and a stile in the corner.

Once out of the garden, a wide grass footpath keeps to the left-hand side of the field and then runs along the top hedgerow to a stile. On this section of the walk you are surrounded by rolling Devon hills, the coast now out of sight far away to the south.

Continue across another field to the next stile where you step into the lane to the Okenbury Estate. **(E)** A signpost still gives Ringmore at 1½ mile to the left, but after 20 yards you reach yet another stile on the right and a sign that corrects the distance to 1¼ mile. Here the farmer has left a wide grass track through the middle of the field. Over the next stile there is a stone and gravel farm track with waymarkers and after 200 yards keep your eyes peeled for the point where the footpath turns left. **(F)** This is shown by a yellow arrow on the gatepost. At the bottom of the field the path bears right alongside a small copse, eventually turning left down through the trees to the valley below. The floor of this wood is carpeted in bluebells in springtime.

You reach the pine trees of the Okenbury plantation and come to a stile and a grass meadow. This ancient Devon valley is straight out of a picture book and the footpath runs beside a brook that courses down between willow trees to the ruins of Nodden Mill with a stone bridge over the stream.

Take a deep breath and start the long climb up to Ringmore. The track leaves Nodden Mill, rising up the hill through the copse, and turning right over a stile at the point where a five bar gate bars the way. The grass bank now rises at 45° and the short stiff climb really stretches the calf muscles.

Step over the stile at the top and cross the next field to a kissing gate and from here you can finally see the sea again with Ayrmer Cove away to the right.

Halfway along the next field the path turns left into a small paddock with a kissing gate in the opposite corner. Just one more field to cross and you step out into the lane leading down to the church and the centre of the village.

The road to Challaborough brings you back to the car park.

## WALK 17 WONWELL BEACH

**Distance** 4 miles
**Time** 3 hours
**Grade** 3

From the A379 take the B3392 to Bigbury-on-Sea and Burgh Island. On the sharp left-hand bend at Seven Stones Cross drive straight ahead towards Kingston and at the Y-junction at Langston Cross, take the right-hand fork and follow the signs to the beach.

The walk starts on the banks of the River Erme at the end of the narrow lane leading down to the river from Blackpost Cross. **(A)** Parking on the verge of this lane is very limited.

(Note: If there is no sensible place left to park in the lane, then drive back to Kingston and park carefully in the village taking care not to cause any obstruction. If parking in Kingston proves necessary then the walk will start at **(E)**.)

At low water you can walk to Wonwell Beach along the sands of the estuary. At high tide the coastal path, signposted to Bigbury-on-Sea, is to the left of the slipway. It passes through a small thicket and comes out into a clearing before dropping down onto the beach. Jump the brook that scours the sand and cross to the other side of the beach where the path climbs to a stile.

As you follow the cliff tops and reach the higher ground you get a beautiful panoramic view of the Erme Estuary. Upriver are Wonwell Beach and the river wending its way down the wooded valley from Dartmoor; while on the opposite shore you have the old Coastguard cottages above Mothecombe Beach and the sands of Meadowsfoot Beach beyond Owen's Point. At low water the sand bars stretch out from either shore to the narrow winding channel of the river that is fordable at Mothecombe: at high tide the wide expanse of unbroken water laps the shores, flooding the valley to the tree lines.

The ground now levels out to a wide swathe of tussock grass, the path making its way to

**Stepping it out**

a stile set in a stone wall. **(B)** A National Trust notice declares that you are entering Scobbiscombe Farm land.

(Note: A footpath to Kingston runs from this stile up the hedgerow to the left and if you wish to shorten this strenuous walk to a comfortable stroll, this path goes up the hill to Scobbiscombe Farm Lane and out to Kingston at **(E)**.)

Heading up the grass hillside to The Beacon, The National Trust have set the farm fences above Fernycombe Beach further away from the treacherous cliff edge because of coastal erosion. From The Beacon there are magnificent views eastwards to the next impressive headland of Hoist Point with Meddrick Rocks stippling the sea below. Burgh Island can be seen together with the sandy beaches of Thurlestone and away to the far headland of Bolt Tail. Westward, across the mouth of the Erme, the shoreline advances to far-off Stoke Point and on a clear day the pale, blue-grey coast of Cornwall stretches south to The Lizard.

Continuing on the coastal path from The Beacon you come to a five bar gate and a stile set in a drystone wall and further on a second gate opens the way to the crest of Hoist Point. The story goes that when this area was being mapped a local swarthy was appointed to assist the surveyor. When asked what the headland was called the yokel replied " 'oiyest point" and so it was recorded.

From the highest point the path zigzags its way down the very steep flank of the hillside to Westcombe Beach.

(The next section of the walk is shared with Walk 16.)

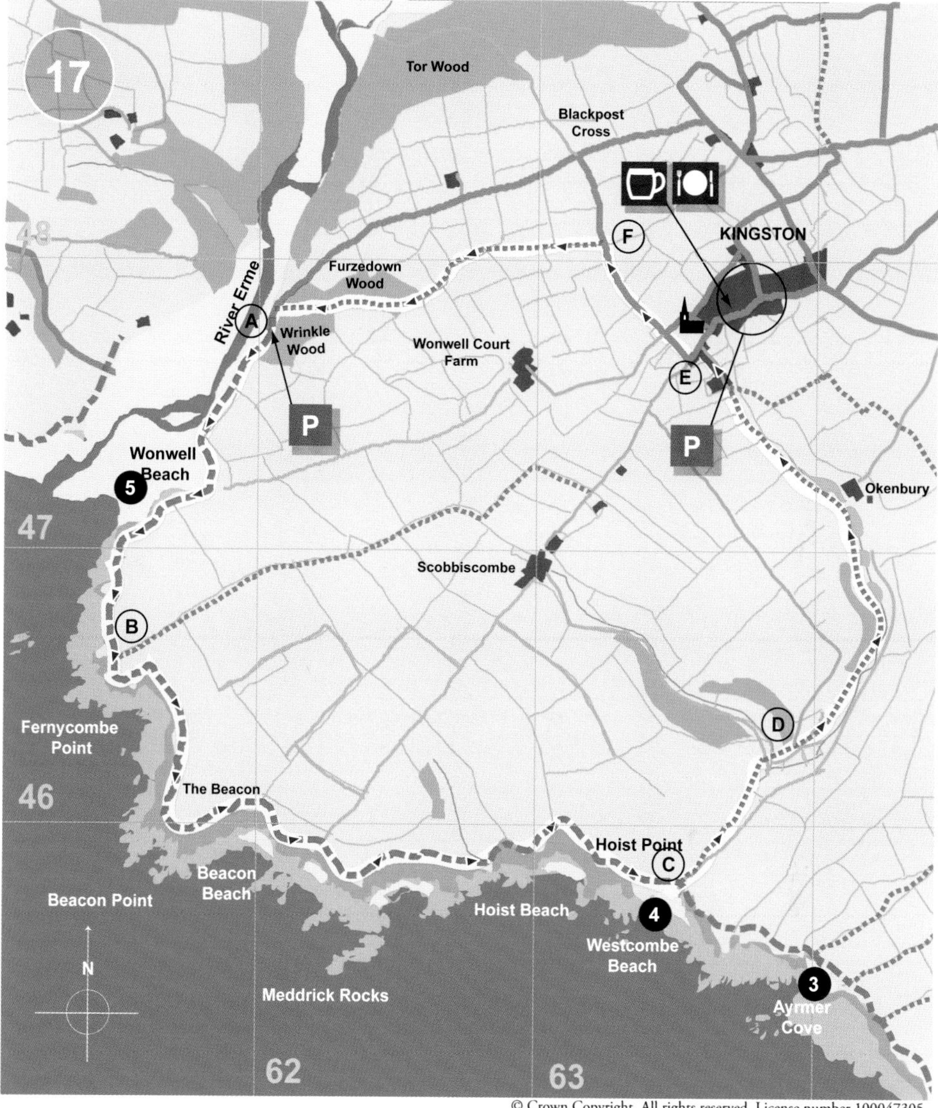




Westcombe Beach is a secluded spot at the head of a valley. **(C)** Take the permissive footpath signposted to Kingston 2 miles. This wide path alongside a stream is a very easy walk up the valley but when you re-cross the stream at a second footbridge the path then starts to climb through a thicket up to a fork in the track. **(D)** Continue on the bridleway to Kingston 1½ miles. The track climbs among woodland and after periods of rain the deep ruts left by farm vehicles can become extremely muddy underfoot. You can hear the tinkling of the stream away to the right as it spills down the valley and as

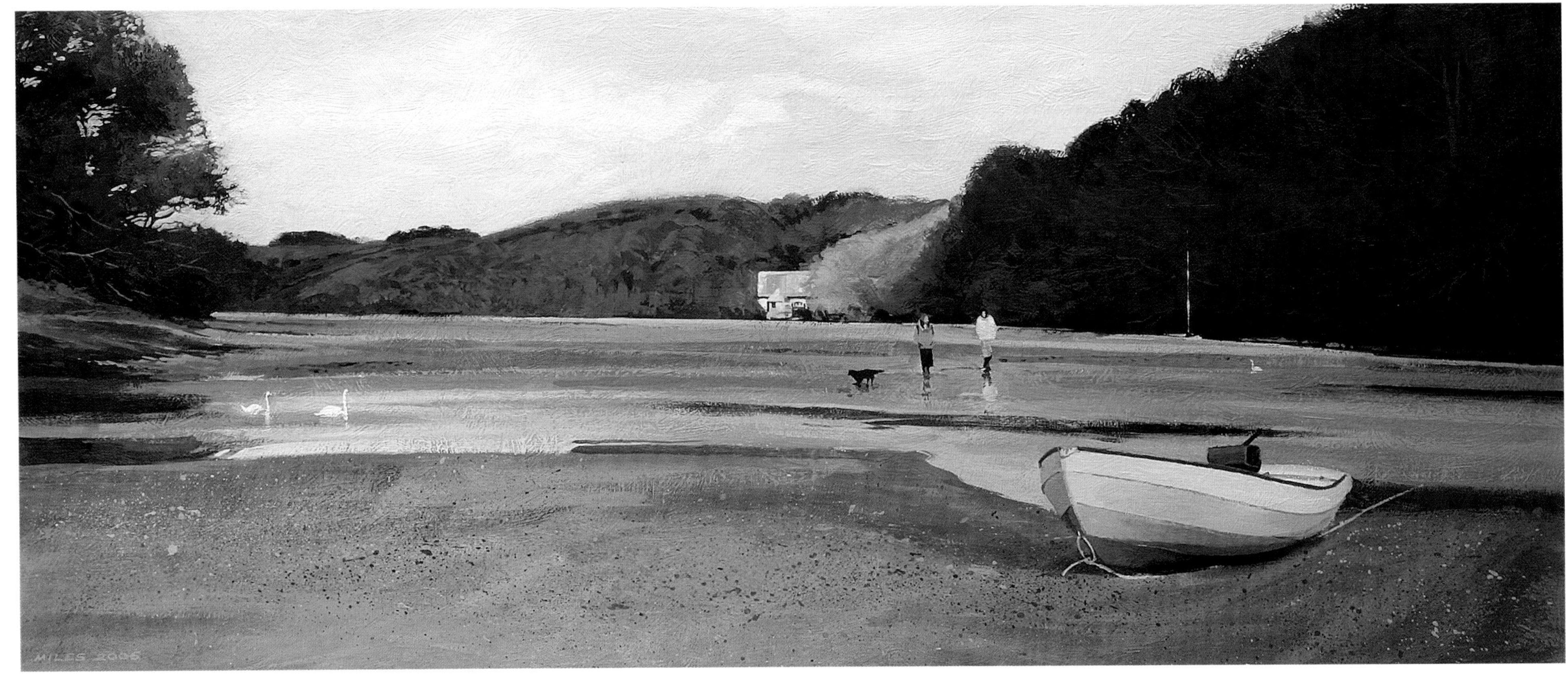


you get closer to Okenbury you pass a series of man-made ponds. At one place a small waterfall separates the pools and there is a crossing with another farm track. Further along, the mill and cottages at Okenbury can be seen through the trees reflected in the waters of a mere, the last and largest of the ponds. Okenbury is a very old medieval estate, The Manor having been mentioned in the Domesday Book.

Less attractive is the Kingston Water Treatment Works at the outskirt of the village where the farm track opens out to a wide gravel road.

Upon entering Kingston you pass the white-painted Walkespool Cottage and as you walk up the rise past the cottage you can check the time against the clock on the tower of Kingston church.

Turn left at the T-junction, walk up the hill past Church Park cul-de-sac and take the next lane on the right. **(E)** ( The blocked lane ahead with signs for a children's play area is the lane to Scobbiscombe Farm, the short cut to this walk mentioned earlier.)

At the next junction go straight ahead leaving Kingston behind.

Immediately after a Z-bend in the lane the public footpath to Wonwell Beach, 1 mile, is signposted to the left. **(F)** There is a stile but at the time of writing there is no gate into the field and the footpath keeps to the left-hand hedge.

Part way along the next field the footpath veers off to the right, crossing the field between the crops, down to the bottom corner. A signpost here clearly directs you over a stile to a sunken footpath between stone walls and high banks.

A series of stiles links the next three fields before you enter Furzedown Wood. It is a well-worn path down through the woodland that during the month of May is carpeted with blue bells. The beaten track comes out into the country lane where you parked your car.

**The River Erme** ▲

As with all rivers flowing from Dartmoor out to sea on the South Hams Coast, the sands at the mouth of the River Erme are subject to constant sculpting from the tidal flow. The narrow channel of this quiet picturesque river weaves a snaking course among exposed flats of sand and gravel that at low water offer a brief opportunity to explore the upper reaches.

# 10 THE RIVER ERME TO THE RIVER YEALM

▲ **Gara Point and the Great Mew Stone**

Gara Point, at the mouth of the River Yealm marks the western extremity of the South Hams Coast. The Great Mew Stone stands off the beach at Wembury and the Cornish coastline stretches away on the far side of Plymouth Sound. A footpath from the National Trust car park close to Blackstone Point brings you out to The Warren and this beautiful windswept view.

## THE COASTLINE

The country road from Holbeton through Battisborough Cross, that narrows to a country lane beyond Eastern Lodge, runs parallel to the coast, but there are few footpaths or farm tracks that link across from this road to the coastal path making this section of the coast quite remote.

From Meadowsfoot Beach at the mouth of the River Erme to Beacon Hill above Stoke Beach there are some serious switchbacks that start with the drop into Bugle Hole, but there is nothing on the scale of the giant roller coaster that pitches over Toby's Point, Hoist Point and The Beacon between Burgh Island and the River Erme. Crumbling cliff edges, with sheer rock faces that plummet to a jagged foreshore and beds of rock that stretch as long fingers into the sea, characterizes this part of the coastline. At low tide these extensive ridges and shoulders of rock are interspersed with sand, but none of the coves are accessible. On calm days the sea looks inviting but with a south westerly swell the rocks soon whip the sea into white foam.

Cattle and sheep graze on the grassland that covers the rolling hills, the patchwork of fields reaching right down to the cliff edge. This smooth undulation is only disturbed by the lichen covered dome of St Anchorite's Rock, a prominent tor that lies below Carswell Farm.

Beyond Stoke Beach, where the rocks seem to erupt upwards out of the sand, the scene softens to grass and gorse covered downs at Stoke Point. The sea shore from here out to Gara Point is still deeply etched by an intricate jumble of rock ledges, broad shelves and gullies that reach far out into the deep water, but the cultivated arable farmland and pastures now stop on the crest of the hills and give way to a natural landscape of gentle gorse covered slopes dotted with sheep that run down to the shoreline. The coastal path is wide and level across the downs and makes for relaxed and comfortable walking with wonderful open views towards Cornwall.

**Looking towards Yealm Pool from Newton Creek**

Gara Point overlooks Wembury Bay and the River Yealm flows out between wooded hillsides, the tidal waters constantly filling and emptying the backwaters and creeks of the estuary, none more beautiful than Newton Creek that separates Noss Mayo from Newton Ferrers.

## ACCESSIBLE BEACHES AND COVES

This section of the South Hams coast is spectacularly rugged but it is very short on bathing places. In fact there are only three that can be sensibly recommended.

**1. Meadowsfoot Beach.**

(Access Level 2)

This is a beautiful sandy beach on the west side of the mouth of the River Erme with safe bathing and a beach available at all stages of the tide with the exception of the highest springs. It is situated on the private Flete Estate but the South West Coast Path runs along the back of the beach above the high water line.

There is a large pay car park in a field at Mothecombe and in the same field during the summer months there is a tearoom in what was once the village school. There are public toilets but on a number of inspections their cleanliness left a lot to be desired.

At the bottom corner of the car park you can step into the lane that leads down to the sandy shores of the Erme Estuary and Coastguards Beach, named after the Coastguard cottages that overlook the estuary. Meadowsfoot Beach can be reached by a footpath to the right of this lane. This crosses private land and a notice states that the Flete Estate allows access to the beach for bathing on Wednesdays and at the weekends.

Dogs are not allowed on the beach from May to October.

**2. Stoke Beach.**

(Access Level 3)

To reach Stoke Beach you must walk through Revelstoke Park. There is a National Trust car park quite a distance away at the mid-point between Stoke Cross and Netton Farm and there is a small visitors' car park at the entrance to the caravan site. A notice in the caravan park requests hikers and bathers to respect the privacy of the park residents by keeping to the footpaths. From the park entrance, take the main driveway down the hill and then the footpath to the beach signposted to the left. Once through the caravan park the footpath runs out to a steel stairway to the beach.

There are no facilities at Stoke Beach and the toilets at the caravan park are for residents only.

**End of a Day's Fishing - Meadowsfoot Beach** ▲

Meadowsfoot Beach is a private beach owned by the Flete Estate on the west side of the mouth of the River Erme. In summer it attracts many bathers and sun seekers but in late autumn the lovely shores of the Erme Estuary are practically deserted apart from a few hikers and fishermen.

▲ **Beacon Hill from Stoke Down**

An off-shore north wind calms the sea on a blustery day in winter, and dark clouds massing inland throw the sunlit coastline into sharp relief. A footpath to the ruins of the church of St Peter the Poor Fisherman at Church Cove runs around the bottom of Stoke Down to this view.

The beach lies at the base of high cliffs and is a mixture of sand, stone and shingle, studded with large rock formations and littered with boulders. In places the rocks are ragged teeth thrusting vertically out of the sand.

Bathing is safe when the sea is calm but care should be taken not to get buffeted against the rocks if the sea is rough. Apart from a small patch of dry sand at the base of the stairway there is no beach to speak of at high tide.

Dogs must be kept on the lead when walking through the caravan park.

**3. Cellar Beach.**

(Access Level 3)

This beach can be reached by walking the coastal path from Noss Mayo towards Gara Point or in the opposite direction from The National Trust car park for The Warren above Blackstone Point.

**Resting the oars**

The footpath to Cellar Beach starts in front of Battery Cottage that looks out over Wembury Bay from the headland above the mouth of the River Yealm. The path first runs on the level to the cliff edge and then narrows to a stone gulley that dips through the trees widening to a rough path with steps hewn out of the rock. There is a split in the path but it is only the right-hand track that goes down to the beach, coming out to a grass area with a wooden bench dedicated to " The swimmers and lovers of Cellars". Here you turn left down some more stone steps bringing you to the rocky foreshore where the mandatory life buoy hangs on a post. This is a wide shelf of rock that makes an excellent diving platform at high water when the beach disappears. At low tide the sand and shingle beach widens out across two small crescent shaped coves. Above the furthest cove water spouts down the cliff from a brook that has been ducted through a pipe.

The cove faces west to the Great Mew Stone and the deep water channel for yachts plying in and out of the Yealm crosses in front of the beach.

## THE RIVER YEALM

The "Yam" as it is pronounced locally is 15 miles long and rises on Dartmoor in an area called Stall Moor. The Estuary is a flooded river valley and the tidal waters reach 4 miles inland. The river twists and turns between steep, wooded hills before flowing out into Wembury Bay where the entrance to the estuary is protected by a bar that dries out at low water. These features combine to make it very difficult to navigate the river under sail without powered assistance.

The estuary is managed by the River Yealm Harbour Authority and moorings for visiting yachts are provided upstream of Yealm Pool beyond where Newton Creek merges with the river. The RYHA allows no noise or disturbance from jet skis or waterskiing in the estuary and in April each year a harbour cleaning operation is organised to keep the waterways, moorings and quays shipshape.

There has been a long tradition of oyster growing in the Yealm even as far back as Elizabethan times and the present day Yealm oyster beds are one of the largest producers in Devon. In the 1970s the oyster beds were completely destroyed by the use of anti-fouling paint used to protect the hulls of yachts and after a ban on this substance it took some 20 years for the oyster business to recover.

Fishing for sea trout is permitted between May and September and salmon fishing takes place from October to December.

## WALK 18 St ANCHORITE'S ROCK

**Distance** 2¾ miles
**Time** 1¾ hours (one way)
**Grade** 3

Exploration of the South Hams coastline would not be complete without walking the South West Coast Path between Beacon Hill and Meadowsfoot Beach at the mouth of the River Erme. Circular walks can be done along this attractive stretch but they involve a lot of tramping along roads and lanes. If you can entice someone to go with you it is best approached as a two car walk. Leave one car at the car park in Mothecombe and drive with the second car to The National Trust car park at Stoke Point. (See Walk 19.) Alternatively you could park carefully in the lane between Eastern Lodge and Caulston where a footpath runs out to Beacon Hill.

It is recommended to start the walk from Beacon Hill **(A)** since the views and outlooks are more spectacular walking eastwards. If you are starting from The National Trust car park then the route description for Walk 19 can be used up to the point that the walk turns inland at Beacon Hill.

Climb over the stile on the east side of Beacon Hill and go down the very steep grass hillside into the valley and cross the valley floor to a gate and stile. The stile is for a footpath that runs down to the low cliffs above Wadham Rocks and Wadham Beach. The beach is a tiny patch of sand between the rocks exposed at low tide but is not worthy of a separate mention as an accessible beach.

The coast path then climbs between gorse bushes past a compound of old sheep pens and after the second stile a track to the left links to the coast road. Going straight on there follows a level stretch above Ryder's Hole and the going is comfortable until you reach the valley between Saddle Rock and the tor of St Anchorite's Rock. **(B)** Here a waymarker directs you down into the valley that has a long brake of trees and a stone wall running down the middle. The path is steep but there are steps cut into the hillside. The sheltered easterly side of this headland is covered in gorse, shrubs and trees. At the bottom of the steps is a five bar gate and a stile and you step over into the field. Along the stone wall to the left a broken culvert spouts running water that a thirsty dog would welcome.

Climb the grass slope on the other side of the valley up to St Anchorite's Rock. (An anchorite is a kind of religious hermit but how the tor got this fanciful name is not known.)

The path passes under the base of the tor and a waymarker points the direction across the next two fields. Below at low tide long fingers of rock run out into the sea separated by strips of sand and gravel but the shore lies below high cliffs and is completely inaccessible

The coastal path then rises and skirts around the sheer walls of Gull Cove. Here the rock strata run in vertical lines down the cliff faces to their base. These treacherous cliffs have sharply etched crumbling edges close to the path and you can gaze down into the deep chasm.

Continue on beyond Gull Cove following the fence line of the field along the cliffs and descend into Bugle Hole. A rough path drops into the valley and then flattens out on grass. A signpost announces "Bugle Hole". The valley behind rises up to Battisborough House surrounded by mature trees on the skyline.

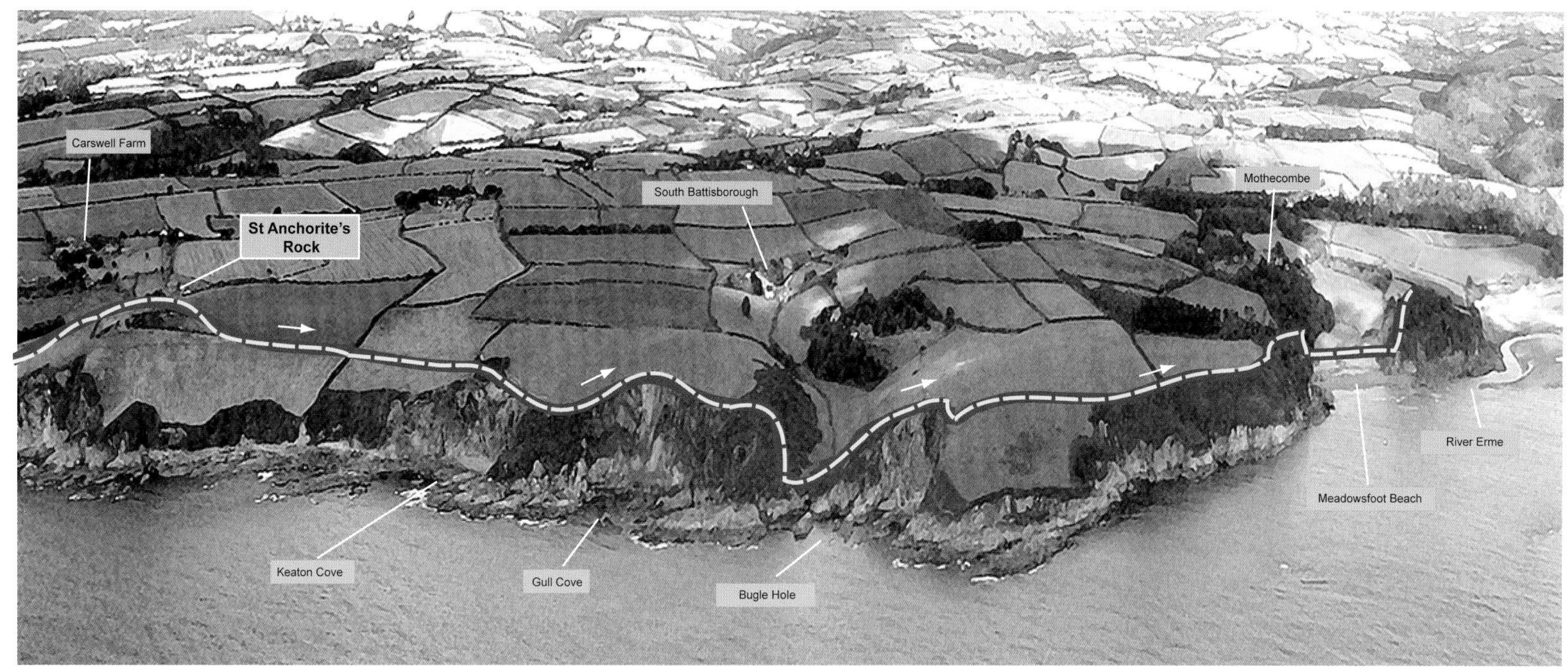


There is quite a stiff climb to the crest of the next hill but from here the path across the following two fields to Meadowsfoot Beach is level. Although there is no indication, the coast path stays inside the fence.

There is a copse of trees running down the left of the second field and ahead is a beautiful old pine tree. Over the hedge to the right you can see Wonwell Beach on the opposite side of the Erme Estuary and the coastline out to Beacon Point.

Beyond the stile the footpath wends its way through the copse down to Meadowsfoot Beach **(C)** and on the other side of the beach you take the footpath to the left to Mothecombe car park.

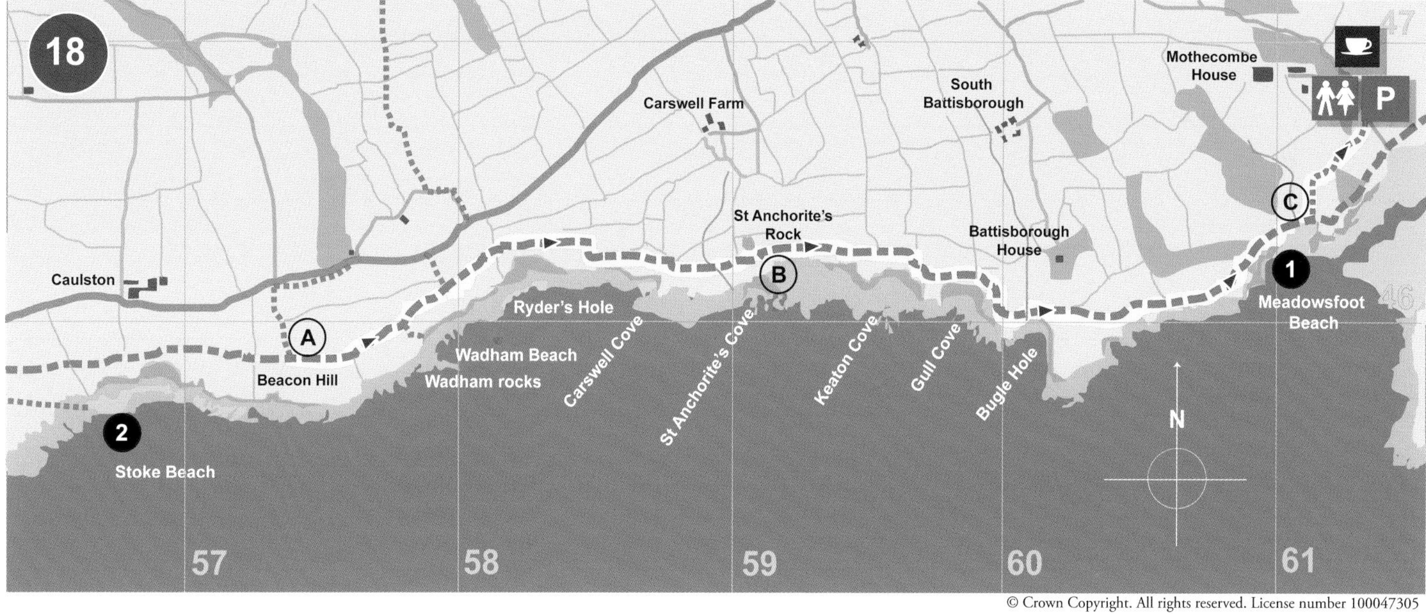

## WALK 19 BEACON HILL

| | |
|---|---|
| **Distance** | **4¾ miles** |
| **Time** | **3¼ hours** |
| **Grade** | 2 |

Follow the signs to Netton from Bridgend in Noss Mayo and at Netton Farm turn left at the T-junction, the car park is 200 yards on the right.

The walk starts at The National Trust car park for Stoke Point. **(A)**

A grass and stone track leads from the car park out towards the coast and as you reach the brow of the hill a vista opens to the left of Bigbury Bay spreading right away to Hope Cove and Bolt Tail, and to the right the coast runs west across Gara Point at the mouth of the River Yealm. At the end of the track a footpath drops down the grass bank to the coastal path where you turn left passing through a second gate towards Stoke Point.

The grass hillside sloping down to the rocky foreshore is Netton Down and since the downs are constantly used for sheep grazing, dogs must be kept under control.

The footpath to the right **(B)** descends the side of Stoke Down to the ruins of the church of St Peter the Poor Fisherman and takes you around the base of Stoke Down into Revelstoke Park. You may choose to continue along the coastal path, since both paths meet up again at the caravan park entrance.

Keeping to the coastal path you round the headland and exit Stoke Point by another gate.

From here the path is sheltered on the seaward side by a small copse of old gnarled trees covered in lichen and clad in ivy and each side of the path is blanketed with brambles. During the winter you catch glimpses of the caravans below but it does not detract from the walk. Coming out of the trees you have a clear view of Stoke Beach and Beacon Hill with its distinctive small ruin on top, and a little further on you step through a gate into the visitors' car park of Revelstoke Park. **(C)**

Beyond Stoke House the coastal path is signposted to the Erme Estuary. The farm track narrows to a grass footpath and you step over a brook. After the next five bar gate and kissing gate, the shrub brake gives way to open downs but the path remains sheltered from sea breezes by a line of hawthorn bushes. Looking back the caravan park is clearly visible.

The footpath up to Beacon Hill now becomes exposed as you pass a group of pine tree skeletons on the right. Whether they were subject to disease, hit by lightning or drought they must have been very impressive in their prime. A small group of healthier trees surmounts the top of Beacon Hill together with the ruins of a small house; a few stubs of wall and an arch remain. This is possibly the house that Lord Revelstoke built for his wife, where she painted watercolours of the surrounding scenery. Bigbury Bay is spread out in front of you with Burgh Island in the middle distance.

Over a stile at the side of a five bar gate

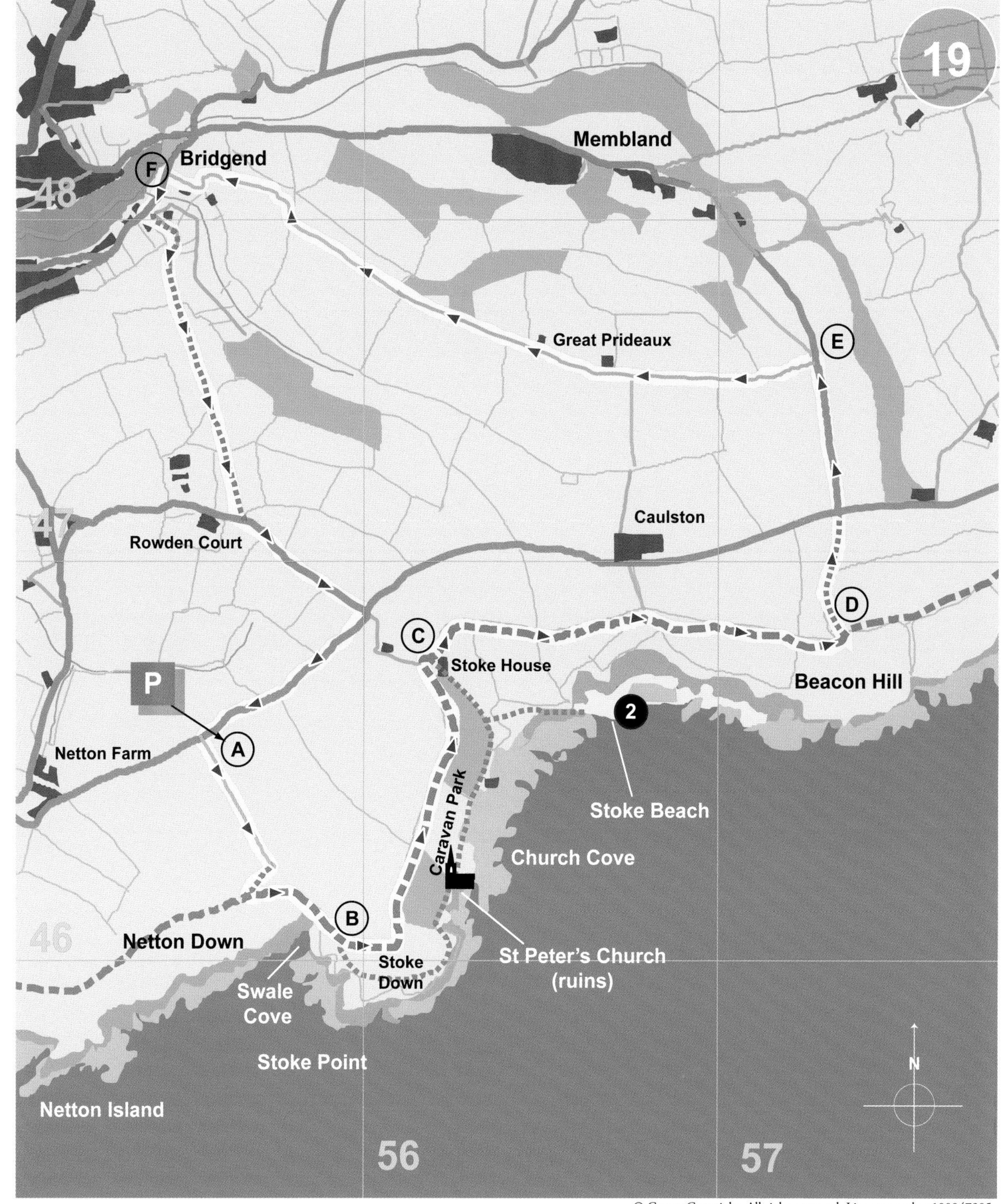

MILES 2005

**St Peter's Church - Revelstoke**

There are two churches called St Peter's in the parish of Noss Mayo. One is prominently perched on a hill above the village looking out over Newton Creek and the other is a ruined chapel tucked away among trees on the rocky shore in the middle of Revelstoke Park at Stoke Beach.

The ruined chapel was once the parish church and dates from Anglo Saxon times. It is a mystery as to why this chapel was built in such a remote spot, but perhaps there was once a small settlement here that was either destroyed by storm or erosion or even came under attack from the sea. The chapel was itself badly damaged by a storm in 1840.

The parish church of St Peter's in Noss Mayo was built by Lord Revelstoke in 1882 to replace the derelict chapel which is now known as the church of St Peter the Poor Fisherman. These ruins are maintained by The Devon Historic Churches Trust which has carried out major repairs to the walls and roof. The church and graveyard are open to the public.

◄ **Noss Mayo**

Newton Creek is a branch of the Yealm Estuary that separates Newton Ferrers on the north shore from Noss Mayo to the south. At high tide the boats float serenely at anchor reflected in the calm water, but they lay stranded in mud with their masts at jaunty angles when the ebbing tide almost completely drains the creek. The mature woodlands that cover the surrounding hills reach down to the water's edge, their lowest outstretched branches squarely trimmed at the high water line.

you enter the area of Beacon Hill and on the other side the coastal path marches on across the downs towards the River Erme.

This is where the walk breaks from the coast and turns inland. **(D)** A stile gives access to a footpath that crosses two fields to a gap in the far hedgerow. This pastureland is often grazed by a large herd of cows, so keep dogs on the lead. Although this is a public footpath, this farmer has a tendency to bar the way with electric fencing. Take care to grip the insulated handle firmly before uncoupling the electric wire from the fence! Reconnect it once you are through.

Cross the road and follow the lane opposite signposted to Memblands. As you walk along the lane Dartmoor rises before you showing the white scars of the china clay quarries. After 200 yards turn left into the lane to Great Prideaux Farm, **(E)** to the right the white-painted cottages of Membland stand out on the ridge and beyond these cottages is the river valley that runs down to Newton Creek. The tarmac road ends at the farm and deteriorates to a deeply rutted farm track that in winter can be very muddy with deep puddles. After 50 yards the track dries and starts to descend to Noss Mayo; across the valley you can see the rooftops of Newton Ferrers. The track peters out to a footpath and a wonderful view of Newton Creek is gained from the farm gate at the top of the rise just where the tree lined footpath disappears down the hill.

At the bottom of the hill the driveway from Creek Cottage comes out at Bridgend and the main road to Noss Mayo. **(F)** The walk goes along the road to the left but before moving on take a break and cross the road to the gravelled area to the right of the row of buildings that face the creek. Here you find a seat and the most picturesque view of Newton Creek dominated by St Peter's Church. At low tide egrets and ducks forage in the mud.

Walk along the road for 100 yards and take the footpath to the left just after you pass the entrance to the boat quay on the right. There are house signs for "Rowan Orchard" and "Three Corners" on the stone wall. A yellow arrow on the gatepost of Three Corners points the way to the footpath to the right. The path follows the edge of the field.

Now starts the stiffest climb of the walk. The footpath zigzags its way up through a copse around the back of Rowan Orchard and ends at a stile. The arrow on the stile directs you straight up the steep grass bank but in fact you must walk diagonally up the field to the left. The footpath is not clear, but as you make your way up the left-hand side of the field you eventually come to a gap in the hedge with a gate and a stile. The footpath is now more clearly defined and it crosses the next two fields diagonally, the fields being separated by yet another stile. From the second field you enter the lane by Rowden Court, a large impressive country house and converted barns complex.

The National Trust car park is now in view and having climbed over the stile, walk left up the lane to the T-junction and then right along the coast lane to the car park.

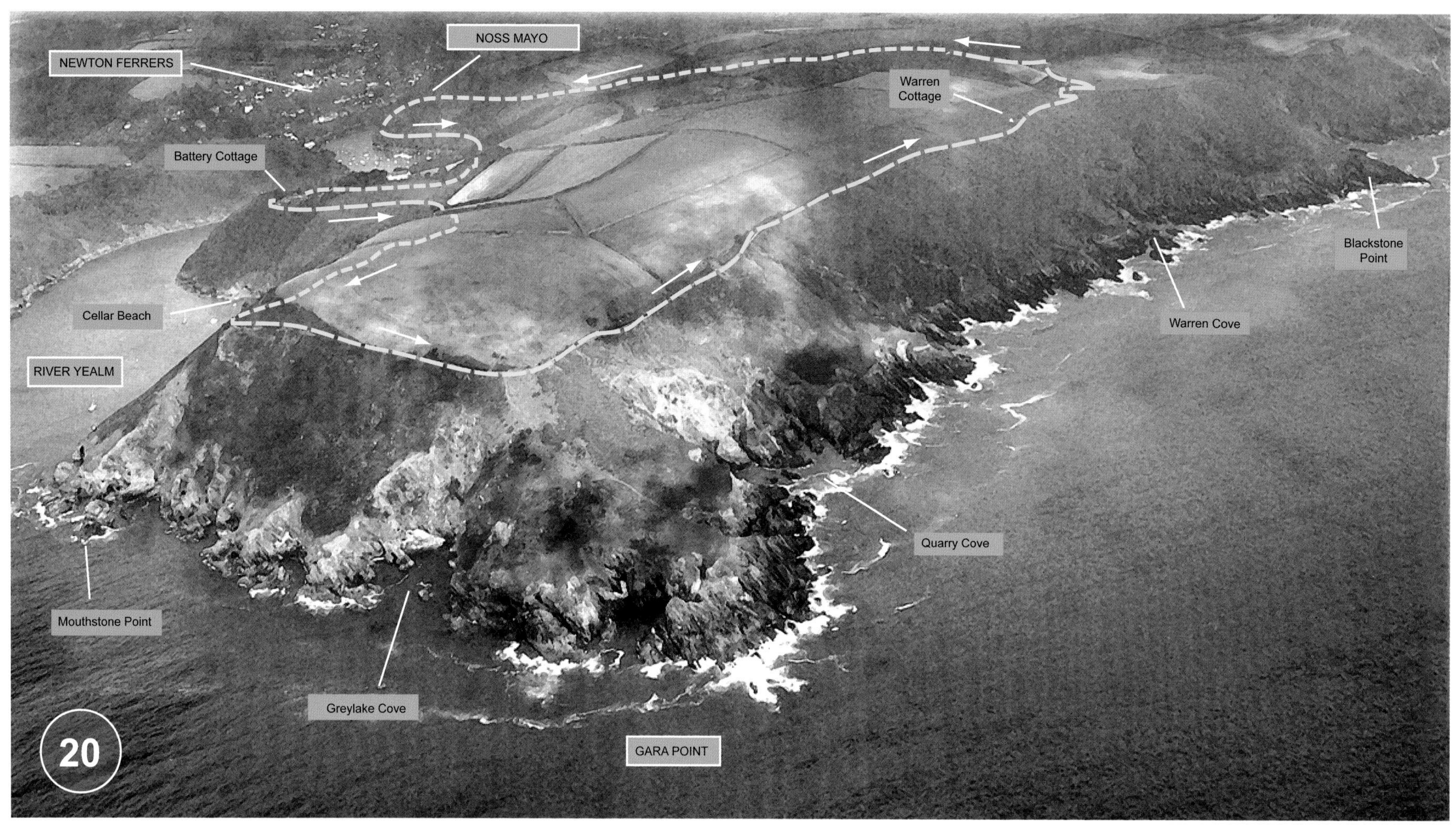


**WALK 20 NOSS MAYO**

| | |
|---|---|
| **Distance** | **4 miles** |
| **Time** | **2½ hours** |
| **Grade** | **1** |

The walk starts at The National Trust car park for The Warren. **(A)** The easiest way to reach this car park is from Bridgend at Noss Mayo following the signs to Netton and Worswell.

Leave the car park and go back into the lane and turn left. Immediately on the right is a farm track marked "Private Drive – No Parking" and a signpost showing that it is a public footpath to Noss Mayo. This is a wide cinder track that wends its way downhill between fields and hedgerows. After you pass a small, neat farm with houses made of natural stone the track becomes a little rougher and is ridged in the middle with grass.

The path comes out at the top of Noss Mayo nestling in the valley below. The parish church of St Peter's stands on top of the hill to the right.

Go down past the tennis courts and a small public car park that could be used as an alternative starting point for this walk. Follow Foundry Lane to the head of Noss Hard, with its shingle beach. **(B)** The building on the right with the tiny bell tower was originally called the Chapel of Ease that later became the school and has ended up as the village hall.

There is also parking here on both sides of the creek but if you choose to start the walk from this point, make sure you park above the high water line if you want to avoid any surprises when you return to your car!

The Ship Inn and The Swan face each other across Noss Hard and if you time the walk carefully you could arrive here for lunch. On a sunny day the terraces of these two pubs are perfect settings in which to relax and soak up the ambiance of this charming backwater

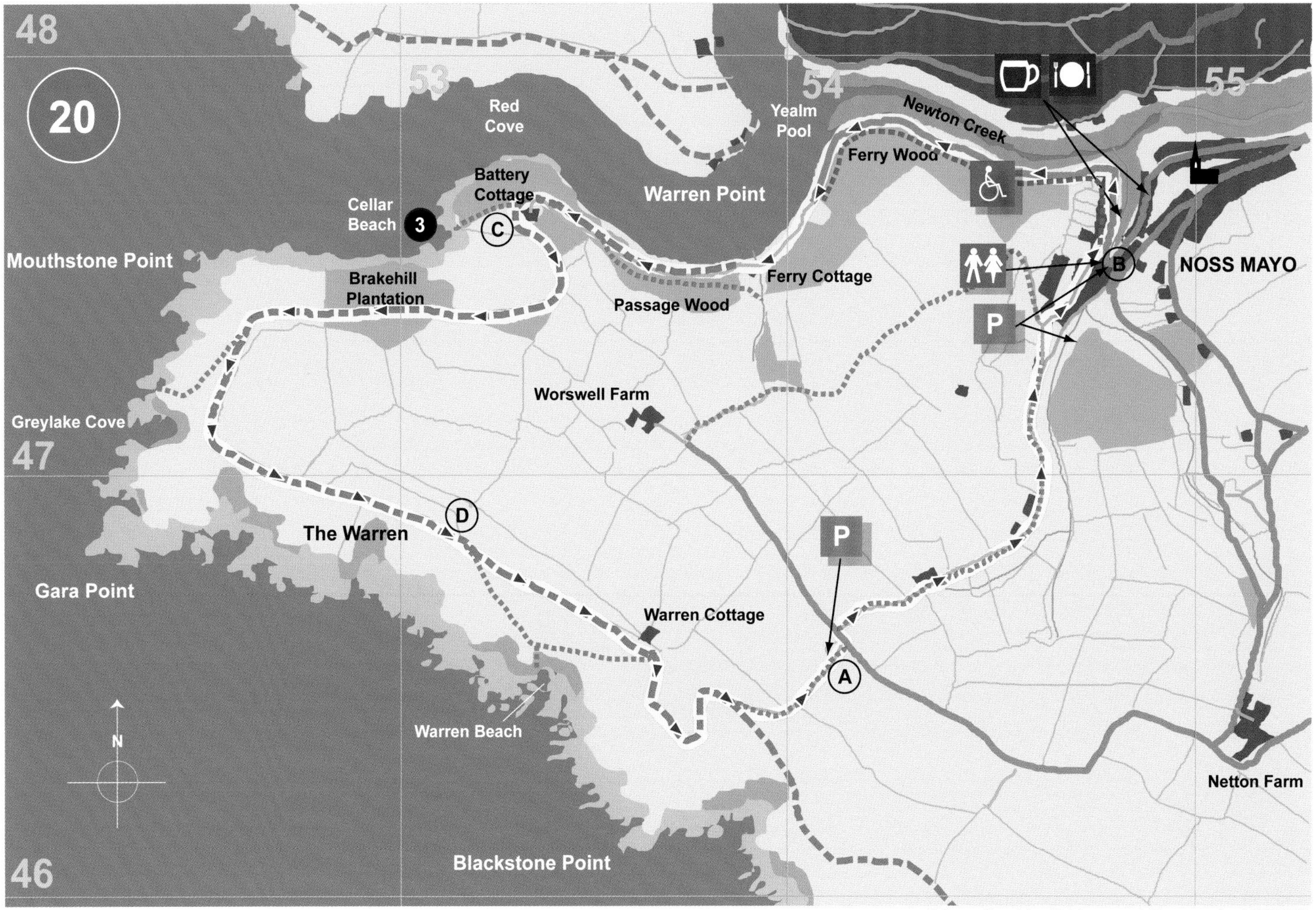

Take Passage Road that passes behind the Ship Inn and walk out to Newton Creek. This road is bordered on the left by a row of attractive cottages that looks across to Newton Ferrers on the opposite side. The road turns left at Point Cottage and at the end of the road you leave the village under a canopy of trees as you enter The National Trust area of Ford Hill Plantation. In contrast to the natural woodlands on this side of Newton Creek the houses of Newton Ferrers are arranged in terraces on the opposite hillside and extend right along to the end of the creek where it joins the River Yealm.

You pass Wide Slip where the seasonal Yealm Ferry plies its trade between Noss Mayo, Newton Ferrers and Warren Point throughout the summer months. From Warren Point you can pick up the South West Coast Path to Wembury Beach and beyond to Plymstock.

A signpost points the way onwards to Stoke Beach 5 miles and here the River Yealm curves widely around Warren Point and out to sea into Wembury Bay. Kilpatrick Steps go down to a small jetty and at low tide it is possible to walk along the stone, gravel and sand foreshore.

The coastal path splits away from the road off to the right, signposted to Stoke 4¼ miles and the road straight ahead up the hill goes through Passage Wood. This is the practical limit for disabled people in wheelchairs, since the coastal path is impassable and the upper track starts to climb and the road surface becomes much rougher.

The coastal path crosses a small brook before turning right in front of Toll House that displays a board showing the old tolls and dues that were payable to the Yealm Ferry in the days of yore. A gravel path then goes up to a gate by Ferryman's Cottage and opens out to a woodland path that rises through the tree-lined hillside to rejoin the wider road. In the winter the river can be glimpsed through the tracery of bare branches but in summer the dense foliage blankets the views.

Here a notice states that parking will only be tolerated at the roadside provided access is left clear for emergency vehicles. There is a turning point further along by a five bar gate but this area is not recommended for use as parking for the walk. There are few passing places along Passage Road and it should be left free for those people who need to use it.

Next to the five bar gate a display board from The National Trust welcomes you to Passage Wood and maps out the circular walk that you are following, with the exception that their route does not include the waterfront at Noss Mayo. The track now serves as a driveway to Battery Cottage and a group of converted Coastguard cottages on the headland above Cellar Beach. **(C)**

The SHIP INN
MILES 2005

You walk around Battery Cottage with its beautiful weathervane of a galleon, mounted on top of an attractive square tower with slate roof and leaded windows. After the Coastguard cottages a gate opens to the next stage of the walk. Before going on just take the time to lean on the five bar gate on the right and contemplate the view out to the Great Mew Stone. ("Mew" is old English for seagull).

Cross the stream that runs down the field on to Cellar Beach that provides a good watering hole for the dog and walk on up to Brakehill Plantation and out to the bare shoulder of Gara Point. Here benches are positioned to enjoy the panoramic view encompassing the entrance to Plymouth Sound and the far coastline of Cornwall; to the right the stubby square tower of St Werburgh's Church at Wembury can be seen above the beach.

Rounding the point the scene changes to the wide open seascape of the English Channel. The gorse covered slopes of The Warren roll down to short-cropped grass ledges above the bare rock teeth of the foreshore. The walk along the coast to Blackstone Point is on a high, wide, level track known as Revelstoke Drive. You may decide to take the detour down to Warren Beach below the remote Warren Cottage, the track is to be found 50 yards beyond the second kissing gate. **(D)** To call it a beach is a bit of a misnomer as it consists of sharp rocks interspersed with shale. The display board of The National Trust suggests that it is a place to watch for porpoises and whales. Steps in the rock face drop down to the "beach".

The climb back brings you out just beyond Warren Cottage.

Revelstoke Drive then takes a wide curve around the back of Blackstone Point where an abandoned shepherd's hut stands forlornly on the summit of the next headland. Pass through the gate in a stone wall and then turn left following the signs back to the car park.

◄ **The Ship Inn**

The Ship Inn is a waterside pub on Noss Hard, a small inlet of Newton Creek at Noss Mayo. It is popular with both yachtsmen and hikers. From here you can walk out along the Yealm Estuary to Gara Point, continuing back along the coastal path to Blackstone Point. From here public footpaths thread inland and down a valley back to the village.

**Lord Revelstoke.**

Edward Charles Baring was appointed 1st Baron Revelstoke of Membland in 1882. He was the senior partner of Baring Brothers Merchant Bank and Director of the Bank of England from 1879 to 1891.

As Lord of the Manor he was an important benefactor for Noss Mayo having built the parish church of St Peter's and other buildings in the village.

The wide coastal path from Noss Mayo that passes around Gara Point, crosses The Warren and continues out to Blackstone Point is known as Revelstoke Drive. This was a driveway that he had cut from the hillside so that he and his guests could enjoy horse-drawn carriage rides along the coast from Membland Hall to the village.

**Cottages at Bridgend**

**The River Yealm** ▲

The River Yealm is at its widest as it sweeps majestically around Warren Point before flowing out into Wembury Bay. Viewed from the quay on the Newton Ferrers' side of the river, the woodland blanketing the hills on the far shore forms an imposing backdrop, the darkened foliage impenetrable against the shimmering reflection of the afternoon sun on the swirling water.

# INDEX OF PAINTINGS

**Kingsbridge Waterfront** ▲

The water is mirror-still on this peaceful winter's morning. Yachts are hauled up onto the quayside for storage and the 'River Maid', ferrying tourists between Salcombe and Kingsbridge throughout the bustling summer months, rests at her moorings.

# INDEX OF WALKS

## INDEX OF ACCESSIBLE BEACHES AND COVES



## INDEX OF HIGHLIGHTED FACTS